The Tao of Natural Breathing

Also by Dennis Lewis

Free Your Breath, Free Your Life (book)

Natural Breathing (audio)

THE TAO OF
NATURAL BREATHING

For Health, Well-Being
and Inner Growth

Dennis Lewis

RODMELL PRESS, BERKELEY, CALIFORNIA • 2006

Library of Congress Cataloging-in-Publication Data is available.
Permissions are on page 187.

Printed in China
First Edition
ISBN-10: 1-930485-14-X
ISBN-13: 978-1930-48514-3
10 09   3 4 5

Cover Design: Gopa & Ted2, Inc.
Book Design: Ingalls & Associates
Book Designers: Caroline Byrne and Thomas Ingalls
Illustrations: Juan Li
Lithographer: Kwong Fat Offset Printing Co., Ltd.

A WORD OF CAUTION

The practices in this book are not intended to replace the services of your
physician, or to provide an alternative to professional medical treatment.
This book offers no diagnosis of or treatment for any specific medical
problem that you may have. Where it suggests the possible usefulness of
certain practices in relation to certain illnesses or symptoms, it does so
solely for educational purposes—either to explore the possible relationship of natural breathing to health, or to expose the reader to alternative
healing approaches from other traditions, especially the Taoist tradition
of China. The breathing practices outlined in this book are extremely gentle, and should—if carried out as described—be beneficial to your overall
physical and psychological health. If you have any serious medical or psychological problem, however—such as heart disease, high blood pressure,
cancer, mental illness, or recent abdominal or chest surgery—you should
consult your physician before undertaking any of these practices.

Text set in New Baskerville 9.5/14

Distributed by Publishers Group West

Dedicated to my son, Benoit, who, from the moment of his birth, has inspired me to always attempt to keep learning and growing.

And with my most profound gratitude to Lord John Pentland, my primary teacher, who was an outstanding leader of the Gurdjieff Work in America until his death in 1984, and who taught me how to think from the perspective and sensation of wholeness; Jean Klein, the Advaita Vedanta master who helped me understand that love and consciousness are at the very heart of being; and Mantak Chia, the Taoist master who brought the Healing Tao to America, and who, along with Chi Nei Tsang practitioner Gilles Marin, showed me that healing is a power we all have—the creative power of life itself.

CONTENTS

Empty yourself of everything.

Let the mind become still.

The ten thousand things rise and fall while the Self watches their return.

They grow and flourish and then return to the source.

Returning to the source is stillness, which is the way of nature....

Lao Tsu, *Tao Te Ching*

FOREWORD

There is a growing interest today in the relationship of breathing to health and spiritual development. Unfortunately, few people who experiment with their breath understand the importance of "natural breathing." This is the kind of spontaneous, whole-body breathing that one can observe in an infant or a young child. Instead of trying to learn to breathe naturally, many people impose complicated breathing techniques on top of their already bad breathing habits. These habits are not in harmony with the psychological and physiological laws of the mind and body. They are not in harmony with the Tao.

Natural breathing is an integral part of the Tao. For thousands of years Taoist masters have taught natural breathing to their students through chi kung, tai chi, and various other meditative and healing arts and sciences. Through natural breathing we are able to support our overall health. We are able to improve the functioning and efficiency of our heart, lungs, and other internal organs and systems. We are able to help balance our emotions. We are able to transform our stress and negativity into the energy that we can use for self-healing and self-development. And we are better able to extract and absorb the energy we need for spiritual growth and independence.

Many books on breathing have been published over the past several years. None of them, however, has gone as deeply into the meaning, practice, and benefits of natural breathing as this important new work by Dennis Lewis. Based on his own long study and research in various traditions and disciplines, including the Healing Tao, Lewis brings together in one book the psychosomatic vision, the scientific knowledge, and the vital practices that can help us discover the power of natural breathing to rejuvenate and transform our lives.

The Tao of Natural Breathing makes a big contribution to our understanding of how the way we breathe influences our lives. Whatever their level of experience, readers will gain new insights into their own specific breathing habits and how these habits often undermine their health and well-being. They will understand that natural, authentic breathing depends less on learning new breathing techniques than it does on what Lewis calls the "reeducation" of our inner perception. This reeducation, which involves learning how to sense the inner structures and energies of the mind and body, lies at the heart of the Taoist approach to healing and spiritual development.

MASTER MANTAK CHIA
The International Healing Tao
Chiang Mai, Thailand

William Blake wrote: "There is a crack in everything that God has made." For me, this crack—this place where something new and more meaningful can enter our lives—became especially visible in 1990, when I found myself physically, emotionally, and spiritually exhausted, with a constant, sharp pain on the right side of my rib cage. I had just gone through the enormous stress of selling my public relations agency to a well-known English firm, and had worked to maximize the sale price of the company for two years under the direction of the new owners. Though I had had chronic abdominal discomfort for many years, and indeed had been diagnosed with "colitis" some years before, this pain was different. I went to doctors, massage therapists, and various body-work practitioners to put an end to it, but to no avail. It was during this period that I met Gilles Marin, a student of Taoist master Mantak Chia, and a teacher and practitioner of Chi Nei Tsang (CNT), a Taoist healing practice using internal-organ chi massage and work with breathing to clear unhealthy tensions and energies from our bodies.

When Gilles first put his hands into my belly and began to massage my inner organs and tissues, and when he began to ask me to breathe into parts of myself that I had never experienced through my breath, I had no idea of the incredible journey of discovery that I was beginning. Though Gilles told me that CNT was part of a larger system of healing and spiritual practices called the "Healing Tao," founded by Master Chia, my immediate concern was simply to get rid of the pain. I had my own spiritual practices; what I needed was healing.

Healing. ... A word I had not pondered very deeply in my life. But as Gilles began to work more intensively with me, and as it became increasingly clear that the healing process depended in large part on my own inner awareness, I began to understand why the expressions "to heal" and "to make whole" have the same roots. Though the physical pain disappeared after several sessions, and though I began to feel more alive, a deeper, psychic pain began to emerge—the pain of recognizing that in spite of all my efforts over many years toward self-knowledge and self-transformation, I had managed to open myself to only a small portion of the vast scale of the physical, emotional, and spiritual energies available to us at every moment. As Gilles continued working on me, and as my breath began to penetrate deeper into myself, I began to sense layer after layer of tension, anger, fear, and sadness resonating in my abdomen below the level of my so-called waking consciousness, and consuming the energies I needed not only for health, but also for a real engagement with life. And this deepening sensation at the very center of my being, painful as it was, brought with it an opening not only in the tissues of my belly, but also in my most intimate attitudes toward myself, a welcoming of hitherto unconscious fragments of myself into a new sense of discovery, wholeness, and inner growth.

I quickly realized that Chi Nei Tsang—with its penetration into my physical and emotional energies through touch and breathwork—provided a direct, healing pathway into myself, and as I learned more about it through its action on me I soon found myself taking classes from Gilles and even beginning to work on my friends. I also found myself taking classes in healing practices and chi kung, many of which involved special breathing practices, from various Healing Tao teachers, including Master Chia. After more than a year of CNT classes and many hours of clinical practice, I was tested by Master Chia and certified by him to do CNT professionally. And after many Healing Tao classes and retreats, as well as intensive work on myself, I also became certified by Master Chia to teach some of the Healing Tao practices. Since then I have done CNT work both on my own clients and at a Chinese medicine clinic in San Francisco, and have taught ongoing Healing Tao classes and workshops, with a large emphasis on breathing.

As a result of my work with the Healing Tao, as well as with other teachings, such as the Gurdjieff Work and Advaita Vedanta, two facts have become clear to me with regard to the relationship of breath to health and inner growth. First, that our poor breathing habits have arisen not only out of our psychosomatic "ig-norance," our lack of organic awareness, but also out of our unconscious need for a buffering mechanism to keep us from sensing and feeling the reality of our own deep-rooted fears and contradictions. There is absolutely no doubt that *superficial breathing ensures a superficial experience of ourselves.* Second, that if we were able to breathe "naturally" for even a small percentage of the more than 15,000 breaths we take during each waking day we would be taking a huge step not only toward preventing many of the physical and psychological problems that have become endemic to modern life, but also toward supporting our own inner growth—the growth of awareness of who and what we really are, of our own essential being. It is my hope that the ideas and practices explored in this book will help make this possible.

A Miracle and a Warning

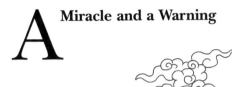

   The process of breathing, of the fundamental movement of inspiration and expiration, is one of the great miracles of existence. It not only unleashes the energies of life, but it also provides a healing pathway into the deepest recesses of our being. To inhale fully is to fill ourselves with the energies of life, to be inspired; to exhale fully is to empty ourselves, to open ourselves to the unknown, to be expired. It is through a deepening awareness of the ever-changing rhythms of this primal process that we begin to awaken our inner healing powers—the energy of wholeness.

   To breathe is to live. To breathe fully is to live fully, to manifest the full range and power of our inborn potential for vitality in everything that we sense, feel, think, and do. Unfortunately, few of us breathe fully. We have lost the capability of "natural breathing," a capability that we had as babies and young children. Our chronic shallow breathing reduces the working capacity of our respiratory system to only about one-third of its potential, diminishes the exchange of gases and thus the production of energy in our cells, deprives us of the many healthful actions that breathing naturally would have on our inner organs, cuts us off from our own real feelings, and promotes disharmony and "dis-ease" at every level of our lives.

   What is natural breathing? How would this kind of breathing alter our lives and our health? To answer these questions we must undertake an experimental study of breathing in the laboratory of our own body. We must personally experience how our breath is intimately bound up not just with our energy, but with every aspect of our being—from the health of our tissues, organs, bones, muscles, hormones, and blood to the quality and breadth of our thoughts, attitudes, emotions, and consciousness. We must begin to understand the great power that our breathing has to help open us or close us not only to our own inner healing powers but also to our potential for psychological and spiritual development.

Of all the great ancient and modern teachings that have explored the full significance of breath in our lives, the Taoist tradition of China, which is more a way of life than a formal religion, offers one of the most practical and insightful approaches to the use of breath for health and well-being. One of the reasons for this is that from the very beginning of Taoism, at the time of the reign of the Yellow Emperor (Huang Ti) around 2700 B.C., the goals of health and longevity were never separated from the goals of spiritual evolution and immortality. Taoists realized that a long, healthy life filled with vitality is not only an intelligent goal in its own right but also an important support for the more difficult goal of spiritual growth and independence. Supported by more than 4,000 years of experimentation with their own physical, emotional, mental, and spiritual energies through special postures and movements, massage, visualization, sound, meditation, diet, and many other practical disciplines, the Taoists observed that natural breathing—breathing according to the actual "laws" of the human organism—could have a powerful influence on the quantity and quality of these energies and thus on the quality and direction of our lives. For if the Tao can be defined at all, it means *the way*, the laws, of nature and the universe—the laws of creation and evolution. It is through living in harmony with these laws that we become free to discover and fulfill our physical, psychological, and spiritual destiny.

The Tao of Natural Breathing integrates key Taoist teachings and practices regarding breath—especially those arising through my work with Taoist master Mantak Chia—with my observations and discoveries over the past 30 years in relation to various other systems and teachings, including the Gurdjieff Work, Advaita Vedanta, Feldenkrais®, and Ilse Middendorf, as well as with important principles from anatomy, physiology, and neurochemistry. It is my experience that any serious work with breathing requires far more than appropriate exercises. It also requires a clear "scientific view" of the human body and a deep work of organic awareness—the ability to sense and feel oneself from the inside.

A WARNING ABOUT BREATHING EXERCISES

The great spiritual pathfinder G. I. Gurdjieff once said that "without mastering breathing nothing can be mastered."[1] But he also warned that without complete knowledge of our organism, especially of the interrelationships of the rhythms of our various organs, efforts to change our breathing can bring great harm. It is clear that work with breathing, especially some of the advanced yogic breathing techniques (pranayama) taught in the West through both classes and books, is fraught with many dangers. In his book *Hara: The Vital Center of Man*, Karlfried Durckheim—a pioneer in the integration of body, mind, and spirit—discusses some of the dangers of teaching yogic breathing techniques to Westerners. He points out that most of these exercises, which "imply tension," were designed for Indians, who suffer from "an inert letting-go." Westerners, on the other hand, suffer from "too much upward pull ... too much will." Durckheim states that even though many yoga teachers try to help their students relax before giving them breathing exercises, they do not realize that the "letting-go" required for deep relaxation can be achieved "only after long practice." At best, says Durckheim, giving breathing exercises prematurely grafts new tensions onto the already established ones, and brings about "an artificially induced vitality ... followed by a condition of exhaustion and the aspirant discontinues his efforts, his practice."[2]

Based on my own work on myself, as well as on my observation of others, I believe that it is only after many months (or even years) of progressive practice rooted in self-observation and self-awareness that most Westerners can experience the deep inner relaxation, the freedom from willfulness, needed to benefit in a lasting way from advanced breathing exercises—whether yogic, Taoist, or otherwise. Breathing exercises involving complicated counting schemes, alternate nostril breathing, reverse breathing, breath retention, hyperventilation,[3] and so on make sense only for people who already breathe *naturally*, making use of their entire body in the breathing process. It is my experience that natural breathing *is in itself* a powerful form of self-healing. That is why *The Tao of Natural Breathing* explores this kind of breathing in so much depth, describing in detail some fundamental perspectives and practices that can, through increased inner awareness, help us see and transform our own personal obstacles to its manifestation in our lives.

One could say, of course, as some Taoist masters and other teachers have said, that since natural breathing is natural, *any effort* to breathe naturally both misses the point and is counterproductive. They maintain that when our mind becomes calm and empty, natural breathing will arise automatically.[4] Accepting this assertion, however, does not solve the problem; it simply puts us in front of another question: what are the conditions that allow us to calm and empty our minds? What personal work is needed? It is no use to shift the problem from the body to the mind or from the mind to the body. Natural breathing involves the participation of both.

The appearance of natural breathing in our lives is not just a matter of what we do, but also—and perhaps more importantly—of how we do it. If we approach the practices in this book as mere techniques to be manipulated by our so-called will, they will bring us nothing. If, however, we can approach them as natural vehicles to explore the physiological and psychological laws of our mind and body—through direct impressions coming from an inner clarity of awareness—we may in fact begin to learn what it means to calm and empty our minds. No matter how we live or what we do (or don't do), we are always doing something; we are always practicing something—if only mechanically repeating and further entrenching the narrow, often unhealthy, habits of mind, body, and perception that shape our lives. To gain real benefit from the practices in this book, then, we must approach them as consciously as possible, taking care to *understand* their aim, *feel* their spirit, and *sense* their effect on our entire being.

EXPANDING OUR NARROW SENSE OF SELF

The real power of the ideas and practices described in this book is to help us first experience and then free ourselves from the many narrow, unconscious attitudes we have about ourselves and the world—attitudes that create stress and other problems for us in almost every area of our lives. It is often these very attitudes—deeply entrenched in our minds, hearts, and bodies, and manifested through and supported by our breathing—that diminish our awareness, constrict our life force, and prevent us from living conscious, healthy lives in harmony with ourselves, with others, and with our environment.

Fortunately, we do not have to try to deal with each of these attitudes individually—an impossible task in one lifetime. Like spokes radiating out from the central axle of a wheel, our attitudes radiate out from the axle of our own particular self-image: the narrow, incomplete, yet strong image of self, of "I," that permeates almost everything that we think, feel, and do. According to Lao Tzu, if we can somehow expand this narrow image we have of ourselves and live from our wholeness, then many of our problems will disappear on their own:

> What is meant by saying that the greatest trouble
> is the strong sense of individual self
> that people carry in all circumstances?
> People are beset with great trouble
> because they define their lives so narrowly.
> If they forsake their narrow sense of self
> and live wholly, then what can they call trouble?[5]

To see and free ourselves from our own "narrow sense of self" is to begin to become open to the tremendous healing forces and energies that create and maintain our lives—to experience for ourselves how the alchemical substances of matter and the magical ideas of mind are linked in the unified, transformative dance of yin and yang—the dynamic polarity of opposites from which all life springs. It is also to experience here and now the return to the primal, expansive emptiness and silence of "wu chi," the all-inclusive wholeness that is the source of both our being and our well-being. It is our breath that can help guide us on this remarkable journey into ourselves.

THE MECHANICS OF BREATHING

*The process of breathing,
if we can begin to understand it
in relation to the whole of life,
shows us the way to let go
of the old and open to the new.*

The process of breathing is a living metaphor for understanding how to expand our narrow sense of ourselves and be present to the healing energies that are both in and around us. Every time we inhale we take in some 10^{22} atoms, including approximately one million of the same atoms of air inhaled by Lao Tzu, Buddha, Christ, and everyone else who has ever lived on this earth. Every time we exhale, we return these atoms to the atmosphere to be renewed for both present and future generations. Every time we inhale, we absorb oxygen expelled into the atmosphere as a "waste product" by the earth's plant life. Every time we exhale, we expel carbon dioxide as a "waste product" into the atmosphere where it can eventually be absorbed by this same plant life. In nature, nothing is wasted. Our breath is a link in the cosmic ecology—in the conservation, transformation, and exchange of substances in nature's complex metabolism. It connects our so-called inner world with the vast scale of the outer world—of the earth and its atmosphere, as well as of all organic life—through the perceptible alternation of yin and yang, of negative and positive, of emptying and filling. The process of breathing, if we can begin to understand it in relation to the whole of life, shows us the way to let go of the old and open to the new. It shows us the way to experience who and what we actually are. It shows us the way to wholeness and well-being.

SOME PERSONAL HISTORY

In my own case, breathing took on a special, historical significance for me long before I understood why. As a child I had a tremendous fascination with holding my breath. Lying in bed, I would often hold my breath for two minutes or so before finding myself gasping for air. As a young adult, the moment I started wearing suits I realized that I was troubled by the sensation of a tight collar or a tie around my neck. It was only later, when I was in my early thirties, that my mother told me I had been a breech baby, and that the doctors had fully expected me to come into the world dead, strangled by the umbilical cord wrapped tightly around my neck. Indeed, it was wrapped around my neck, but I was still able to breathe, still able to take in the precious nectar that we call air.

It is obvious to me today, however, that my 30-hour struggle to reach light and take my first breath left deep impressions in my body and nervous system, and laid the foundation for some of the fundamental fears and insecurities that have often motivated my behavior as an adult. It is obvious to me today also that this deeply entrenched belief that only through persistence and struggle could I somehow find meaning and happiness in my life—a mode of behavior which served me well during birth, as well as during my childhood and teenage years—became an obstacle to my health and psychological growth as I grew older. All of this has become clearer as my breathing has begun to give up its restrictive hold on my sensory and emotional awareness, expanding into more of the whole of myself.

THE NEED FOR CLARITY AND MINDFULNESS

What is the relationship of our breath to our experience of ourselves and to real health and well-being? What is the relationship of our breath to our quest for self-knowledge and inner growth? To begin to answer these questions in a way that can have a long-lasting, beneficial impact on our lives, it is not enough to go to a weekend rebirthing or breathing intensive, or to simply start doing exercises from a magazine or book. Because of the intimate relationship between mind and body—the many subtle yet powerful ways they influence each other—any lasting, effective work with our breath requires *clear mental knowledge* of the mechanics of natural breathing and its relationship to our muscles, our emotions, and our thoughts. The clarity of this picture in our mind will help us become more conscious of our own individual patterns of breathing. It is through being "mindful" of these patterns that we will begin to sense and feel the various psychophysical forces acting on our breath from both the past and the present. And it is through the actual observation of these forces in our own bodies that we will begin to see how we use our breathing to buffer ourselves from physical and psychological experiences and memories too difficult or painful to confront. And, finally, it is through this entire process—the integration of mental clarity with sensory and emotional awareness—that we will begin to experience the extraordinary power of "natural breathing" and its ability to support the process of healing and wholeness in our lives.

THE ANATOMY OF BREATHING

For most of us, our cycle of inhalation and exhalation occurs at an average resting rate of 12 to 14 times a minute when we are awake, and six to eight times a minute when we are asleep. A baby breathes at about twice these rates. Our breathing rates can change dramatically in relation to what we are doing or experiencing. Under extreme physical activity or stress, for example, the rate can go up to 100 times a minute. For those who have worked seriously with their breath, the resting rate can go down to four to eight times a minute, since they take in more oxygen and expel more carbon dioxide with each inhalation and exhalation.

The Chest Cavity and Lungs

The process of breathing takes place mainly in the chest cavity, the top and sides of which are bounded by the ribs (which slant downward and forward) and the attached intercostal muscles, and the bottom by the dome-shaped muscular partition of the diaphragm (Figure 1). Inside this cavity lie the heart and the two lungs. Shaped somewhat like pyramids, the lungs are divided into three lobes on the right and two on the left. The lobes are composed of a spongy labyrinth of sacs, which, if flattened out, would cover an area of approximately 100 square yards. The lungs are covered by the pleura, a double-layer membrane lining the inside of the ribs, and are supported by the diaphragm. Extremely elastic, the lungs are free to move in any direction except where they are

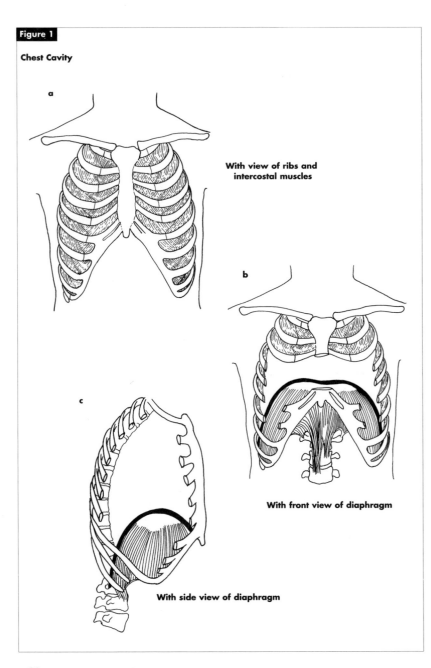

Figure 1

Chest Cavity

a

With view of ribs and
intercostal muscles

b

With front view of diaphragm

c

With side view of diaphragm

attached through tubes and arteries to the trachea and heart. Though the lungs have a total air capacity of about 5,000 milliliters, the average breath is only about 500 milliliters. Though, as we shall see, we can learn to exhale much more air than we normally do, no matter how fully we may exhale, the lungs always hold a reserve of about 1,000 milliliters of air to keep them from becoming completely deflated. It is easy to see that most of us use a small percentage of our lungs' capacity.

We seldom pay attention to the breathing process in the course of our daily activities, but when we do we can sense the chest cavity expanding and contracting, somewhat like a bellows. During inhalation, the rib muscles (intercostals) expand and elevate the ribs, the sternum moves slightly upward, and the diaphragm flattens downward. The expanded space creates a partial vacuum that sucks the lungs outward toward the walls of the chest and downward toward the diaphragm, thus increasing their volume as air is drawn in automatically from the outside (Figure 2). The air that we inhale is composed of about 20 percent oxygen and .03 percent carbon dioxide; the rest is nitrogen. During exhalation, the rib muscles relax, the sternum moves downward, the diaphragm relaxes upward (regaining its full dome-like curvature), and the old air is expelled upward through the trachea as the lungs recede from the walls of the chest and shrink back to their original size (Figure 3). The exhaled air consists of 16 percent oxygen and 4 percent carbon dioxide. It is saturated with water vapor produced by metabolic activity.

The Movement of Air through the Respiratory System

As air enters our nose, particles of dust and dirt are filtered out by the hairs that line our nostrils. As the air continues on through the nasal passages it is warmed and humidified by the mucous membranes of the septum, which divides the nose into two cavities. If too many particles accumulate on the membranes of the nose, we automatically secrete mucus to trap them or sneeze to expel them. In general, air does not move through the nasal passages equally at the same time. Usually when the left nostril is more open, the right one is more congested and

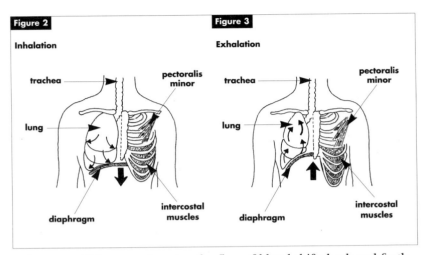

Figure 2

Inhalation

Figure 3

Exhalation

trachea — pectoralis minor

lung

diaphragm — intercostal muscles

trachea — pectoralis minor

lung

diaphragm — intercostal muscles

vice versa. This occurs because the flow of blood shifts back and forth between the nostrils in a rhythm that takes approximately one and a half to two hours.[6]

After passing through the nose, the air then flows down past our pharynx, the cavity at the back of our mouth where the nose and mouth are connected, and where swallowing and breathing are coordinated by the pharyngeal plexus (under the control of the lower brain stem). Here the air passes through the lymphoid tissue of the adenoids and tonsils at the back of the nose and throat, where bacteria and viruses are removed. The air then moves past the larynx, which helps the vocal cords use air to produce sound, and then continues downward into the tube of muscle called the trachea, which separates into two bronchi serving the lungs (Figure 4). The trachea and bronchi are lined with mucus-secreting cells that trap pollutants and bacteria. As the air flows through the bronchi, tiny hairlike lashes called cilia massage the mucus and any remaining debris away from the lungs and upward toward the trachea, over the larynx, and finally into the esophagus. When too many particles, chemicals, or clumps of mucus accumulate in the bronchi, they trigger a coughing spasm—a powerful muscle contraction and bronchial constriction which can generate a

The Tao of Natural Breathing

wind force stronger than a tornado—to expel this toxic material.

In the lungs, the bronchi divide into smaller and smaller branches called bronchioles. The bronchioles, which have muscular walls that can constrict air flow through contraction, end in some 400 million bubble-like sacs called alveoli. It is in the alveoli that the life-giving exchange between oxygen and carbon dioxide occurs—where fresh oxygen enters the circulatory system to be carried throughout the body by hemoglobin molecules in the blood, and where gaseous waste products such as carbon dioxide are returned by the blood for elimination through exhalation.

THE PHASES OF BREATHING

Depending on the demands of what we are doing at the moment (lying down, sitting, walking, running) and on our specific psychological state (peaceful, angry, stressed out, happy), our breath can range from fast to slow and from shallow to deep, emphasizing one or more of the three fundamental phases of the breathing process: *diaphragmatic, thoracic, and clavicular.* In deep breathing, for example—what is often referred to as "the yogic complete breath," all three phases come into play. According to Alan Hymes, M.D., a cardiovascular and thoracic surgeon who is a pioneer in the field of breath research, this form of breathing "is initiated by diaphragmatic contraction, resulting in a slight expansion of the lower ribs and protrusion of the upper abdomen, thus oxygenating the lower lung fields. Then the middle portions of the lungs expand, with outward chest movement, in the thoracic phase as inhalation proceeds further. At the very end of inhalation, still more air is admitted by slightly raising the clavicles, thereby expanding the uppermost tips of the lungs. In sequence, then, each phase of inhalation acts on one particular area of the lungs."[7] As we shall see, no matter what state we may be in, most of us depend mainly on chest and clavicular breathing, and have little experience of diaphragmatic breathing. Thus, we seldom draw air into the deepest areas of our lungs, where most of our blood awaits oxygenation.

Figure 4

The passage of
air into the lungs

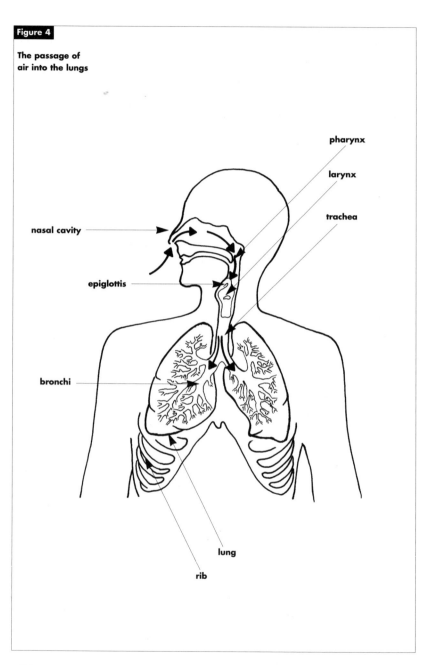

pharynx

larynx

trachea

nasal cavity

epiglottis

bronchi

lung

rib

THE INNER BREATH

Whatever outer form our breath takes, an inner process of breathing also occurs. This process takes place in the cells, which inhale oxygen from the steady stream of hemoglobin flowing throughout the body and exhale carbon dioxide back into this stream. It is in the cells, and more particularly the mitochondria, where the inhaled oxygen helps transform food into biological energy. This transformation occurs when oxygen is combined with carbon (from food) in a slow-burning fire. The energy released from the interaction of oxygen and carbon is transferred to energy storage molecules, called ATP (adenosine triphosphate), which make it available to all the cells of the body. Waste products, such as carbon dioxide, are returned to the venous blood and ultimately to the lungs and back into the atmosphere.

THE RESPIRATORY CENTER

The process of breathing and its relationship to the production of energy in our organism is so fundamental to our survival that nature has given us little direct control over it. Our breathing is thus mostly involuntary, generally controlled by the respiratory center of the autonomic nervous system—especially the vagus nucleus in the medulla oblongata, the nervous tissue at the floor of the fourth ventricle of the brain (Figure 5). The respiratory center, which is located near the occiput (where the spine meets the skull), transmits impulses to nerves in the spinal cord that cause the diaphragm and intercostal muscles to begin the process of inhalation. Branches of the vagus nerve coming from this center sense the stretching of the lungs during inhalation and then automatically inhibit inhalation so that exhalation can take place. The respiratory system is connected to most of the body's sensory nerves; hence any sudden or chronic stimulation coming through any of the senses can have an immediate impact on the force or speed of our breath, or can stop it altogether. Intense beauty, for example, can momentarily "take our breath away," while pain, tension, or stress generally speeds up our breathing and reduces its depth. We can, of

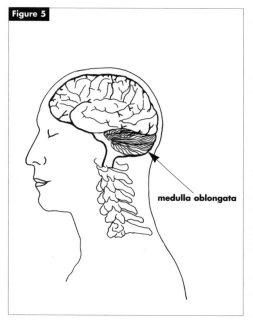

Figure 5

medulla oblongata

course—within limits—intentionally hold our breath, lengthen or reduce our inhalation and exhalation, breathe more deeply, and so on. When we do so, the nerve impulses generated in the cerebral cortex as a result of our intention bypass the respiratory center and travel down the same path used for voluntary muscle control.

Acid/Alkaline Balance

The respiratory center does its work based on the acid/alkaline balance of the blood. The cells in the nucleus of the medulla are sensitive to this balance. From the standpoint of our health, the blood must remain slightly alkaline (pH 7.4). Even tiny deviations from this condition can be dangerous. When the body's chemical activity increases because of physical effort, emotional stress, sensory stimulation, and so on, more carbon dioxide and other acids are produced. This increases the acidity of the blood. To counteract this increase and maintain homeostasis, the respiratory center automatically increases the breath rate. This helps to bring in needed oxygen and to expel excess carbon dioxide. When the body's chemical activity decreases through relaxation or rest, less carbon dioxide is produced and our breathing automatically slows down.[8]

Though we cannot, for the most part, alter the basic chemistry of the respiratory process, we can influence it in a variety of "indirect" ways. One such way is through the relaxation of excessive tension in our postures, movements, and actions. Tension, which involves muscular contraction, produces both lactic acid and carbon dioxide. By reducing chronic tension, we reduce the quantity of these waste products, as well as the work that the body needs to do to counteract them. The relaxation of chronic tension also makes possible the more efficient coordination of the various mechanisms involved in breathing. It is through the harmonious coordination of these mechanisms that we can take in oxygen and expel carbon dioxide with the least possible expenditure of the body's resources.

THE RESPIRATORY MUSCLES

Healthy breathing involves the harmonious interplay not just of the rib muscles, abdominal muscles, and diaphragm, but also of various other muscles throughout the body. These include the extensor muscles of the back, which keep us vertical in relation to gravity, and the psoas muscles, which connect the vertebrae in the lower thoracic and lumbar areas to the pelvis and thigh bones, and are involved in both hip and spinal flexion (Figure 6). Unnecessary tension in the muscles of our shoulders, chest, belly, back, or pelvis—whether it is caused by negative emotions, physical or psychological stress, trauma, injury, or faulty posture—increases the level of carbon dioxide in our blood and interferes with respiratory coordination. It also overstimulates our sensory nerves, which, as we will see later, has an unhealthy influence on our overall functioning.

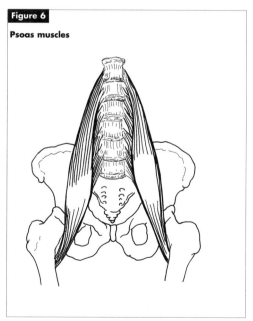

Figure 6

Psoas muscles

The Diaphragm—the "Spiritual Muscle"

Of all the respiratory muscles, the most important from the standpoint of our overall health is the diaphragm. Though few of us make efficient use of this muscle, it nevertheless lies at the foundation of healthy breathing. Shaped like a large dome, the diaphragm functions as both the floor of the chest cavity and the ceiling of the abdominal cavity (Figure 7). It is penetrated by—and can affect—several important structures, including the esophagus, which carries food to the stomach; the aorta, which carries blood from the heart to the arteries of all the limbs and organs except the lungs; the vena cava, the central vein that carries venous blood from the various parts of the body back to the heart; and various nerves including the vagus nerve, which descends from the medulla oblongata and branches to the various internal organs.

Although breathing can continue even if the diaphragm stops functioning, it is the rhythmical contraction and relaxation of the diaphragm that animates our breath and plays an important role in promoting physical and psychological health. When we inhale, the diaphragm normally contracts. This pulls the top of its dome downward toward the abdominal organs, while the various chest muscles expand the rib cage slightly outward and upward. This pumplike motion creates a partial vacuum, which, as we know, draws air into the lungs. When we inhale fully, the diaphragm can double or even triple its range of movement and actually massage—directly in some cases, indirectly in others—the stomach, liver, pancreas, intestines, and kidneys, promoting intestinal movement, blood and lymph flow, and the absorption of nutrients.

Even a slight increase in the diaphragm's movement downward not only has a beneficial impact on our internal organs, but also brings about a large increase in the air volume of the lungs. For every additional millimeter the diaphragm expands, the volume of air in our lungs increases by some 250 to 300 milliliters. Research done in mainland China demonstrates that novices working with deep breathing can learn to increase the downward movement of their diaphragms by an average of four millimeters in six to 12 months. They are thus able to increase the volume of air in their lungs by more than 1,000 milliliters—in a year or less.[9]

At maximum inhalation, the muscles of the abdomen naturally contract to counterbalance the movement of the diaphragm downward and help limit the further expansion of the lungs. As exhalation begins, the diaphragm relaxes upward, its elasticity helping to expel used air from the lungs. When we exhale completely, the diaphragm projects firmly up against the heart and lungs, giving these organs life and support. For Taoist master Mantak Chia, the diaphragm is nothing less than *a spiritual muscle.* "Lifting the heart and fanning the fires of digestion and metabolism, the diaphragm muscle plays a largely unheralded role in maintaining our health, vitality, and well-being."[10]

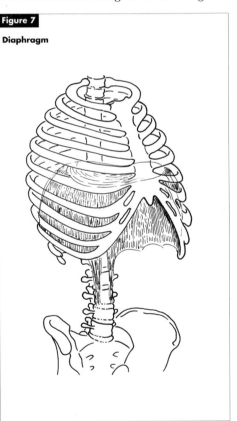

Figure 7

Diaphragm

Restrictive Influences on the Diaphragm

Unfortunately, most of us do not experience the full benefit of this "spiritual muscle." There are two major reasons for this. First, the movement of the diaphragm is adversely influenced by the sympathetic nervous system as a result of the chronic stress, fear, and negativity in our lives (I will discuss the sympathetic nervous system in more detail in the next chapter). Second, it is also adversely influenced by unnecessary tension in our muscles, tendons, and ligaments, as well as by the faulty configurations of our skeletal structure. In understanding this second point, it is useful to know something about how and where the diaphragm actually attaches to the skeletal structure. Though most of the body's muscles are attached to two different bones—one fixed, called the "origin," and one which moves as a result of muscle contraction, called the "insert"—the diaphragm is not attached in this way. The diaphragm is fixed to the inside of the lower ribs as well as to the lumbar spine, close to the psoas muscles, but it does not "insert" to any bone. Rather, it inserts to its own central tendon, which lies just under the heart (Figure 8). The diaphragm is thus influenced by the health and mobility of the spine and pelvis, and their associated muscles, and these in turn are influenced not just by our habitual postures, but also by our emotions and attitudes.

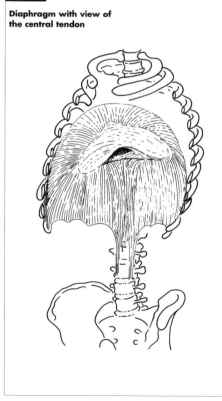

Figure 8

Diaphragm with view of the central tendon

One of the most adverse influences on the movement of the diaphragm is the unnecessary tension that many of us carry in our abdominal muscles and internal organs. Most of these tensions are the result of chronic stress, repressed emotions, and excessive negativity, but they also can be caused by the prevailing image of the hard, flat belly that we find in fashion magazines and fitness centers. When the belly is overly contracted it resists the downward movement of the diaphragm. When this occurs, the diaphragm's central tendon replaces the rib cage and spine as the diaphragm's fixed point, and the contraction of the diaphragm during inhalation causes excessive elevation of the ribs.

Compensating for a Poorly Functioning Diaphragm

To attempt to compensate for decreased lung space resulting from a contracted belly and a poorly functioning diaphragm—especially in times of physical or psychological stress (when more energy is needed)— we either have to breathe faster (which may result in hyperventilation and the emergence of the "fight or flight reflex") or we have to increase the expansion of the thoracic cage and raise the clavicles. Because the thoracic cage and clavicles are relatively rigid, however, this further expansion requires the expenditure of extra muscular effort and energy, and ultimately results in less oxygen being taken in during each breath.

If someone were to ask us to take a deep breath, most of us would make a big effort to suck in our belly, expand our upper chest, and raise our shoulders—a not-so-funny caricature of "chest breathing"—the way most of us breathe most of the time (Figure 9). Such an effort, however, results in a shallow breath, not a deep one. As we shall see more clearly in later chapters, a deep inhalation requires the expansion of the abdomen outward,

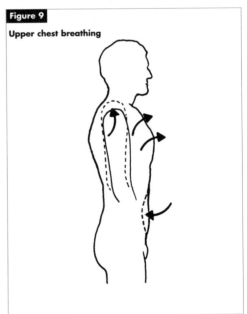

Figure 9

Upper chest breathing

which helps the diaphragm move further downward and allows the bottom of the lungs to expand more completely. Though it is true that raising the shoulders reduces the weight on the ribs beneath and allows the lungs to expand further at the top, the potential volume at the top of the lungs is much smaller than the potential volume at the bottom. Expanding the top of the chest and raising the shoulders may be an effective emergency measure to take in more air for those of us with little elasticity in our diaphragm, rib cage, and belly, or who have asthma or emphysema, but for most of us it only further entrenches our bad breathing habits and undermines our health and vitality.

THE HARMFUL EFFECTS OF BAD BREATHING HABITS

Breathing based on such habits—habits in which the diaphragm is unable to extend through its full range and activate and support the rhythmical movement of the abdominal muscles, organs, and tissues— has many harmful effects on the organism. It reduces the efficiency of our lungs and thus the amount of oxygen available to our cells. It necessitates that we take from two to four times as many breaths as we would with natural, abdominal breathing, and thus increases energy expenditure through higher breath and heart rates. It retards venous blood flow, which carries metabolic wastes from the cells to the kidneys and lungs where they can be excreted before they do harm to the organism. (In this regard, it is important to realize that 70 percent of the body's waste products are eliminated through the lungs, while the rest are eliminated through the urine, feces, and skin.) It retards the functioning of the lymphatic system, whose job it is to trap and destroy viral and bacterial invaders, and thus gives these invaders more time to cause disease. It also reduces the amount of digestive juices, including the enzyme pepsin, available for the digestive process, and slows down the process of peristalsis in the small and large intestines. This causes toxins to pile up and fester throughout the digestive tract. In short, such breathing weakens and disharmonizes the functioning of almost every major system in the body and makes us more susceptible to chronic and acute illnesses and "dis-eases" of all kinds: infections, constipation, respiratory illnesses, digestive problems, ulcers, depression, sexual disorders, sleep disorders, fatigue, headaches, poor blood circulation, premature aging, and so on. Many researchers even believe that our bad breathing habits also contribute to life-threatening diseases such as cancer and heart disease.

Through the gentle, natural practices in this book, however, we can begin to discover the power of natural breathing to counteract these habits and support the overall health, vitality, and well-being that is our birthright.

PRACTICE

The first step to working with your breath is to be clear in your mind about the actual mechanics, the physiological "laws," of natural breathing. This mental clarity will help you experience the breathing process both more directly and more accurately. The next step is to deepen your awareness of your own particular breathing patterns. For your first exercise, read this chapter again; as you read, visualize and sense in yourself the various mechanisms being discussed. Don't try to change anything; just see what you can learn about your own particular breathing process. In the next chapter you'll have an opportunity to go more deeply into the process of self-sensing and its relationship to your breath and health.

little impact. In discussing the importance of attention, an acknowledged master of chi kung and Chinese medicine writes: "By attention we mean both the experience of consciousness and the activity of the brain that lies behind it. Regulating attention allows the practitioner to bring his/her Qi into a comfortable condition. Finding this state of comfortableness and ease is the key to successfully apply Qi Gong to eliminate disease, strengthen the body, prolong life, and promote intelligence."[33] What is crucial in these breathing practices is thus to undertake them with full clarity, effortlessly and comfortably, that is, without strain, without any effort to achieve some result that you think you *should* have. Also give yourself plenty of resting time after each practice, so that you can sense its influence on you.

1 Opening your belly

Sit or stand quietly. Observe how you breathe for several minutes, then put your hands over your navel. As you inhale, sense that you're breathing directly from your nose through a long narrow tube into a balloon behind your navel. As the balloon expands, so does your abdominal area. As you breathe out, the balloon contracts and you have the sensation that the air is squeezed slowly back up through the tube and out through your nose (Figure 14). Obviously, the air that you inhale does not

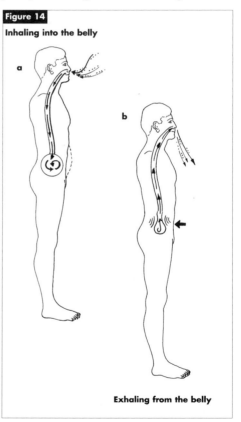

Figure 14

Inhaling into the belly

a

b

Exhaling from the belly

go into the abdomen; it goes into the lungs. But the "sensation" of a movement going from the nose into the abdomen relaxes your abdominal muscles and tissues and helps the diaphragm move lower into the abdomen and massage your inner organs. Be sure that your shoulders and chest remain relaxed during this exercise. *Do not use effort.* Simply visualize and sense the movement of the balloon in your belly. Simultaneously sense the downward and upward movement of the diaphragm as you inhale and exhale.

2 Sensing your diaphragm

To get an even clearer sense of the movement of your diaphragm, lie on your back with your knees bent, your feet slightly apart and flat on the floor, and your arms at your side (Figure 15). As you inhale into your belly, let the balloon expand as much as possible. At the end of the inhalation, hold your breath, making sure that no air can escape through your nose or mouth. Then, without breathing, gradually flatten your belly and gently shift the balloon of air up into your chest. Simultaneously, sense your diaphragm moving upward. Now flatten your chest and shift the balloon back down into your belly. See if you can feel your diaphragm moving downward at the same time. Move the

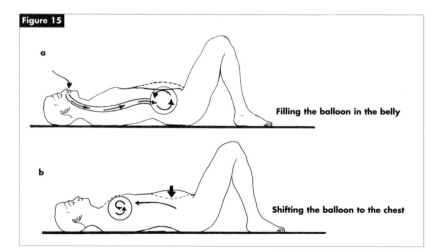

Figure 15

a — Filling the balloon in the belly

b — Shifting the balloon to the chest

balloon back and forth several times in a pumplike motion. Rest for a couple of minutes and observe any changes in your breathing. Try the exercise two or three more times.

3 Opening your rib cage

Continuing to lie on your back, put your hands on the sides of your rib cage over your lower ribs and feel the expansion of the balloon into both sides of the rib cage as you inhale. As you exhale, the ribs return to their normal position. By breathing in this way, you are helping the diaphragm to move even deeper into your abdomen, since the bottom of the diaphragm is attached to the lower ribs. To get an even better sense of the movement of your rib cage, lie on your right side with your head resting on your right arm and your left palm resting gently on the lower left side of your rib cage (Figure 16). As you breathe, feel that you are breathing directly into and out of the left side of your rib cage. Work in this way for 15 or 20 breaths, and then lie again on your back with your feet flat on the floor. Sense your breathing for several breaths—notice if there is a difference between the left and right sides of your rib cage. Now lie on your left side with your head resting on your left arm and your right palm resting on the lower right side of your rib cage. Breathe into the right side of your rib cage for 15 or 20 breaths. Again lie flat on your back with your knees bent, breathe gently into both sides of your rib cage, and sense any changes in your breathing.

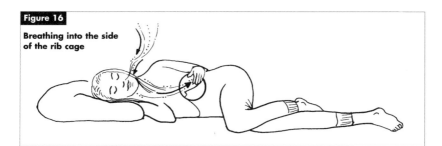

Figure 16

Breathing into the side of the rib cage

4 Opening the "door of life"

Sit or stand comfortably again, putting your hands on each side of your spine on your lower back (tips of the fingers actually touching the spine), directly across from your navel. The Taoists call this area, between the second and third lumbar vertebrae, the "mingmen," or the "door of life," since it is the point between the two kidneys where our sexual essence is stored. It is very important from the standpoint of our well-being to keep this area warm, relaxed, and comfortable. As you inhale, sense the balloon filling and pushing your lower back outward (Figure 17). As you exhale, your lower back returns to its original position. Breathe in this way for two or three minutes. To get the feeling of the movement of your lower back in the process of breathing, try squatting. Squatting is useful not only for opening up the lower back, but also for your overall health. As you squat, let your arms relax forward, and sense your lower back as you breathe (Figure 18). This posture automatically releases the lower back muscles, as well as the lower part of the diaphragm, which is attached to the lumbar spine. It also helps cleanse and energize the kidneys. If you have trouble squatting, you can stand and bend over with your upper body supported by your hands on

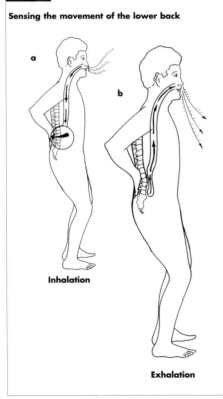

Figure 17

Sensing the movement of the lower back

a

b

Inhalation

Exhalation

your knees. Once you feel the sensation of your lower back expanding and contracting in this way, return to a normal sitting or standing position, and let the "organic memory" of what you just experienced help you sense the same process in this position.

5 Opening the belly, rib cage and lower back simultaneously

Next, either sitting or standing, try to experience all three areas at the same time. Sense the entire space bounded by your navel, your pubic bone, and your lower back. As you inhale, sense the balloon expanding forward, backward, and to the sides more or less simultaneously. As you exhale, sense the balloon contracting. There should be no feeling of effort or tension. Simply sense the balloon filling and emptying. Be sure to sense your diaphragm moving downward as you inhale, and upward as you exhale. After a few minutes, forget the balloon and simply feel the warmth in your abdomen, a kind of ball of energy, expanding and contracting. As you breathe naturally in this way, begin to sense that even though air is not going into the abdominal cavity, "something" is going there. From the Taoist perspective, this something is both blood and chi. By breathing in this way you begin to energize your lower tan tien. You can try this practice several times a day.

Figure 18

Squatting

"ACQUIRED CHI"

The energy that we acquire through food, water, and air is called "acquired chi." This is the energy that we receive from the outside world that we need to function on a daily basis. The main center for the storage and transformation of this energy is the middle tan tien, located in the area of the solar plexus, the center of our emotional life. For the Taoist, the quality of this energy depends in part on the quality of the food we eat and the air we breathe. The Taoist is therefore not only concerned about right diet, but also about right breathing.

As we have seen, proper breathing has many benefits besides the more efficient consumption of oxygen. The practice of abdominal breathing, for instance, has a powerful influence on the digestion of food by increasing gastrointestinal peristalsis, blood flow, and food absorption. It can also help open the tissues around the solar plexus and promote the flow of energy through the channels in this area. According to Mantak Chia, when this area is blocked or energetically weak, we may feel panic or worry, a lack of freedom in our behavior, or an inability to take risks of any kind. We may also feel that we are unloved or incapable of love, or that people are constantly judging us.

Abdominal breathing—especially when it is slow, deep, and long—combined with certain mindfulness practices directed to specific energy centers, can also help us receive the energies of the earth, nature, and the heavens. This form of breathing turns on the parasympathetic nervous system, which calms our brain and body. This allows our inner attention to clearly sense vibrations, impressions, and movements of energies in and around us that are ordinarily invisible to us. It is the sensing of these vibrations, as well as of the centers that can receive them, that allows these energies to be absorbed into our organism.

PRACTICE

1 Opening your solar plexus

Sit or stand quietly and watch your breath for several minutes. Now put your hands over your abdomen and feel the energy ball behind your navel expanding as you inhale and contracting as you exhale. Allow your awareness to go deep inside the tissues in your abdomen. After several breaths, let the energy ball spread, during the inhalation, from your navel area up into your solar plexus (located slightly higher than midway between your navel and the bottom of your sternum). As you exhale, sense the solar plexus and navel areas contracting. As you begin to relax into your inner sensation, your breath will gradually slow down by itself. Put your hands over your solar plexus, and bend over slightly from your waist. See how your breath responds. Repeat this several times. Then stop the bending and bring all your attention to the solar plexus area. Watch how it expands and contracts with each inhalation and exhalation. Work in this way for several minutes.

2 Releasing deep tensions

When you begin to feel your solar plexus becoming more sensitive and open, sense the air going from your nose through your solar plexus and into your lower tan tien (Figure 19). Envision the air as a long thread of silk connecting the whole front of your body from your nose down to your abdomen. As you exhale, breathe out through your mouth. Make sure your mouth is mostly closed, and that your exhalation is slow, quiet, and steady. Allow all the air in your lungs to be exhaled fully before inhaling again. As you exhale, sense that all the tension in your abdomen, solar plexus, and chest is going out through your breath. Breathe quietly in this way for five or 10 minutes. Pay special attention to the area around your solar plexus. Feel it become continually softer, as though something were melting. Then let go of any intention with your breath and simply take note of the various vibrations in and around your body. There's nothing to do but watch and sense. Work for at least 15 or 20 minutes in this way.

SHEN

Shen is generally translated as spirit or higher mind. It is also a substance or energy in the human body. Though shen can be either original or acquired, we will not differentiate it in this book. Sometimes called "celestial chi" because of its origin in the stars, this energy resides in the upper tan tien, the energy center located between the eyebrows in the area of the pituitary gland in the brain (Figure 20). This center controls the basic energy of the mind, the energy required both for clear thinking and for awareness. Shen is the light of lucidity, of consciousness, that shines through our eyes when we are awake. When this area is opened and energized we experience strong intuition and a sense of real purpose. When it is closed or weak, our attention is scattered and we feel distracted or indecisive. There are many stories of Taoist or Chinese doctors who will not treat someone in whom the light of shen is too weak. For without sufficient shen, without a certain level of "spirit," healing becomes impossible.

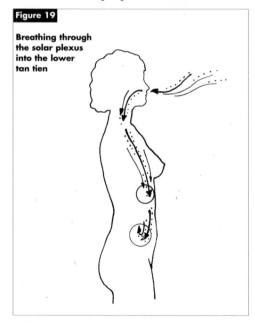

Figure 19

Breathing through the solar plexus into the lower tan tien

Shen Can Be Increased

A certain amount of shen is produced naturally in the organism. But given the various stresses of modern life, it is not always sufficient to keep us healthy, and it is seldom sufficient for psychological or spiritual transformation. But shen can be intentionally increased. One of the best ways to accomplish this is through conserving our basic life force, and supporting the transformation of this life force into the more subtle energy of awareness. This work depends in large part on being able to stay in touch with,

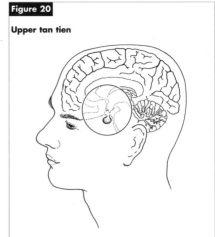

Figure 20

Upper tan tien

to sense, the area of the lower tan tien and learning how to keep this area open and active through awareness and proper breathing. Deep abdominal breathing not only helps move our life force into the higher centers where it can be transformed, but it also helps quiet the mind and calm the brain. This is important because as science has shown, "In the adult, the rate of brain activity, measured metabolically, is ten times that of any other tissue in the body at rest. In fact, the brain burns ten times as much oxygen and produces ten times as much carbon dioxide as the rest of the body."[34]

From both the scientific and Taoist perspectives, the brain's marathon activity influences the entire body, activating nerves, hormones, muscles, tissues, and organs. When the mind becomes quiet—when we can slow down or stop the unnecessary mental and emotional activities (such as daydreaming, criticism, self-pity, inner talking, and random associative thinking) that fill most of our day—the cells and tissues of the brain and body begin to rest and recuperate, spending less energy and storing more. This helps to increase the overall level of energy, of chi, in our organism. When chi reaches a certain level of intensity in the organism, and we are able to sense it through a quiet, ongoing awareness, transformation of more of this energy into the finer energy of shen happens naturally. This higher level of shen not only supports healing and well-being, but is also the foundation for psychospiritual growth.

PRACTICE

1 Opening your brain

Sit or stand quietly in the usual posture, allowing your mind to become quiet and your awareness to include as much of your entire organism and its functions as possible. After 10 or 15 minutes, put your attention just below your navel and sense the energy ball expanding and contracting as you inhale and exhale. Once you feel that you are in touch with this area, allow your attention also to include the upper tan tien between your eyebrows. Sense your eyes relaxing back into their sockets. Feel the entire area around your eyes relaxing. The actual experience feels like something hard softening, or like ice melting to become water. As this melting process takes place, observe any thoughts or feelings you may be having. Don't make an occupation out of these experiences. Let them go, and continue sensing.

2 Breathing into your brain

Once the area between your eyebrows feels soft and open, see if it is possible to inhale directly through this area into your brain, while simultaneously staying in touch with your deep abdominal breathing. See if you can feel a kind of subtle vibration, or movement, in this area. Don't believe the negative thoughts that may arise, thoughts that will undoubtedly tell you that it is impossible to breathe into your brain. Just try it. See for yourself. Work in this way for 10 minutes or so. When you are ready to finish, bring your attention (and your breath) back to your lower tan tien. Feel that any energy you have collected is somehow being stored there. Breathe quietly in this way for a couple of minutes before stopping.

In pondering the implications of the ideas and practices put forward in this chapter, do not worry about remembering the technical terms used here. What is important is to begin to sense that your own harmonious functioning depends on a variety of specific substances (or energies) coming from both inside and outside, as well as on the movement of these substances through your breath to the places in your body where they can be stored and transformed. As you work gently over a period of weeks with the ideas and practices described in this chapter, you will begin to feel a new sense of vitality and openness, especially in your belly, solar plexus, and face. Take note of this sensation. Let it begin to spread throughout your body. Return to it as often as you can.

THE WHOLE-BODY BREATH

... when we are able to breathe through our whole body, sensing our verticality from head to foot, we are aligning ourselves with the natural flow of energy connecting heaven and earth.

More than 2,000 years ago, the great Taoist philosopher Chuang Tzu said that "The True Man breathes with his heels; the mass of men breathe with their throats."[36] This ancient observation about breathing, which may be especially relevant today, lies at the heart of the Taoist approach to breath. For the Taoist, breathing, when it is natural, helps open us to the vast scales of heaven and earth—to the cosmic alchemy that takes place when the radiations of the sun interact with the substances of the earth to produce the energies of life. It is our breath, especially our "natural" breath, that enables us to absorb and transform these energies.

What is "natural" breathing? We began to answer this question in the first two chapters, when we reviewed the basic physiology of breathing and explored how to observe our breath in relation to our tissues and organs. We went deeper into the meaning of natural breathing in the third chapter, when we worked with the three primary energy centers of our body, especially the center in the area of the navel. In this chapter, we will expand the work we've begun to include the whole body in our breath. For it is only when our whole body breathes that we can gain the fullest access to our inner healing power—to the organic vitality that is our birthright.

A SIMPLE DEFINITION OF NATURAL BREATHING

One of the simplest, most practical definitions of natural breathing that I've found comes from the well-known psychiatrist Alexander Lowen, who studied with Wilhelm Reich. "Natural breathing—that is, the way a child or animal breathes—involves the whole body. Not every part is actively engaged, but every part is affected to a greater or lesser degree by respiratory waves that traverse the body. When we breathe in, the wave starts deep in the abdominal cavity and flows up to the head. When we breathe out, the wave moves from head to feet."[37]

From the point of view of this definition, most of us have little experience of natural breathing. In my healing work using Chi Nei Tsang (internal-organs chi massage), for example, many of the people I work on have, at the beginning of my treatments, little awareness of any movement in their abdominal cavity, lower ribs, and lower back. As I observe their breathing, or put my hands into their belly or on their chest, it is clear that the respiratory wave generally begins in the middle of the chest, or even higher, and seems to move only a short distance upward into the shoulders and neck. Some of these people have had abdominal surgery of some kind, and it is clear that even many years later they are still protecting themselves from feeling the pain of the surgery. Others are clearly protecting themselves from feeling painful emotions. Still others feel insecure about their sexuality. But what they all have in common is that they are unconsciously using their breathing to try to cut themselves off from feeling their physical and psychological discomforts and contradictions.

DISTINGUISHING THE OUTER AND INNER MOVEMENTS OF BREATH

To appreciate the true power of natural breathing, it is necessary to begin to distinguish two aspects of our breathing: the outer breath (the way in which our physiology operates to bring about physical respiration) and the inner breath (the subtle breath that circulates throughout our being). Whether we are working alone or being helped by someone with more experience, the key to natural breathing is through training our inner sensitivity, our inner awareness, to sense the various inner and outer movements of our breath as they take place. It is this sensitivity, and particularly its expansion into the unconscious parts of ourselves, that will enable us eventually to begin to sense the physical and emotional forces acting on our breath. It is only when we can sense these forces as they are—without any judgment or rationalization—

that our breath can begin to free itself from its restrictions and engage more of the whole of ourselves.

The Outer Movements of Breath

From what we've said so far, it is possible to discern at least two levels of movement in our respiratory apparatus during inhalation and exhalation. During inhalation, as the air travels downward through our nose and trachea, the diaphragm also moves downward to some degree into the abdomen to make room for the lungs to expand, while the belly expands outward to make room for the diaphragm. Thus the first movement that we can sense in natural breathing is the downward movement of the diaphragm and air. As the lungs begin to fill from the bottom, however, there is also a movement of the air upward—the kind of movement that occurs when we fill a glass or a bottle—which is reinforced by a movement of the chest outward and the sternum upward, creating more room in the middle and upper part of the lungs (Figure 21).

During exhalation, we can sense the air moving upward and out in concert with the diaphragm, which relaxes back into its original dome-like structure pushing upward. Simultaneously, we can sense the movement of the sternum downward and the ribs and belly inward, all of which bring about an overall relaxation of the whole body downward into the earth (Figure 22). Thus, whether we are inhaling or exhaling, we can sense two simultaneous movements going in opposite directions. Indeed, it is through the simultaneous sensing of these opposing movements of air and tissue that we begin to develop the kinesthetic awareness—the inner sensitivity—necessary to relax our tissues and discern the movement of energy in our organism.

The Inner Movements of Breath

From the Taoist perspective, the main issue in natural breathing is the movement of the actual "breath energy," the chi, in the organism. The movement of this energy is the result of the polarity between inhalation (yang, active, upward) and exhalation (yin, passive, downward),

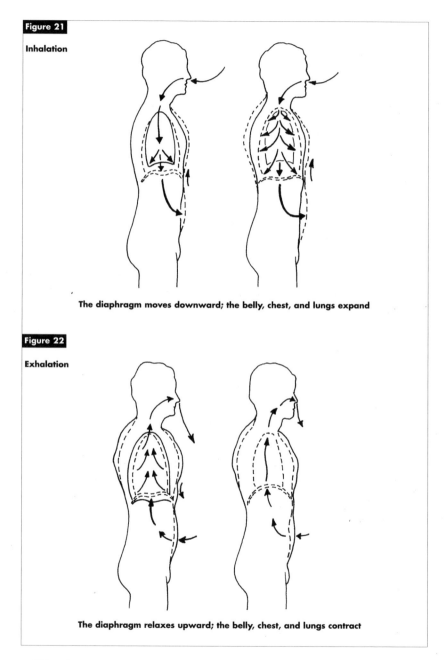

Figure 21

Inhalation

The diaphragm moves downward; the belly, chest, and lungs expand

Figure 22

Exhalation

The diaphragm relaxes upward; the belly, chest, and lungs contract

between filling and emptying. The Taoists have observed that as we inhale, the breath energy moves upward to the head, and that as we exhale, the energy moves downward into the whole body. They have also observed that as we inhale, we can also draw the yin energy of the earth, a powerful healing energy, through our feet and upward into our body. As we exhale, we can direct any toxic or stagnant energies downward to our feet and out into the earth. The Taoists also maintain that during inhalation we can draw the yang energy of heaven directly into our body through the crown, the energy center on the very top of our head, and that during exhalation we can distribute this energy downward throughout our body (Figure 23).

THE POLARITY OF HEAVEN AND EARTH

Whether or not we believe in the energies of heaven and earth, we know that it is the polarity of positive and negative, of yang and yin, that creates electricity and makes energy move. We also know that there are various electromagnetic fields surrounding the earth, and that these fields are themselves manifestations of this fundamental polarity. An American firm that has produced negative ion generators for the space program points out, for example, that a natural electric field exists between the earth and the atmosphere, and that this field—which has a strength of several hundred volts per meter in an open space with unpolluted air—is usually positive in relation to the earth. The company also points out that experiments have shown that this field attracts negative ions from the upper atmosphere and produces an electric current in the body that stimulates living organisms in a beneficial way.[38]

The Taoists, of course, have spoken for thousands of years about the polarity of yang and yin, of up and down, of heaven and earth. As living organisms, we depend not only on chemical and electrical polarities within our bodies, but also on the electromagnetic polarity of the earth and atmosphere. As conductors within this electromagnetic field, our bodies manifest a potential difference in voltage between head (positive) and feet (negative) that increases in relation to the degree of our

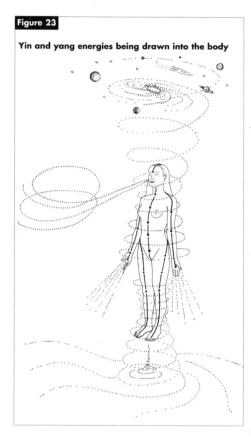

Figure 23

Yin and yang energies being drawn into the body

verticality. Other important factors include our location, the purity of the air, the climate, and so on. In a closed space with polluted air, for instance, the potential difference is virtually zero.

It is my belief that when we are able to breathe through our whole body, sensing our verticality from head to foot, we are aligning ourselves with the natural flow of energy connecting heaven and earth. This vertical flow may help to explain the great healing power of both tai chi and chi kung, especially when they are done, as recommended by Taoist masters, in fresh air and open spaces.

THE BENEFITS OF WHOLE-BODY BREATHING

In addition to bringing us into a more harmonious relationship with the energies of heaven and earth, whole-body breathing has a number of benefits at both the physiological and psychological levels. At the physiological level it not only increases our intake of oxygen and helps to promote efficiency in the entire breathing mechanism, but it also helps—through the internal massage it provides—to revitalize all the cells, tissues, and organs of the body, and to clear the body of any toxins. At the psychological level, whole-body breathing helps us relax enough to begin to experience ourselves from the inside out, to discover an inner attention that can take in more accurate, complete impressions of the whole of ourselves and our functioning. As this occurs—as our breath expands into hitherto unconscious parts of ourselves—our attitudes and emotions start to change and our self-image begins to release its stranglehold on our lives.

PRACTICE

Sit down and go through as many of the previous practices as time permits. When you finish these practices, let your awareness embrace the whole of your sensation. You will feel this sensation—including your skin, your tissues, your muscles, tendons, and ligaments, your organs, and your bones—as varying intensities of vibration, some denser, some finer. See how many levels of vibration you can discern.

1 Sensing the outer movements of breath

Now, within this field of sensation, begin to follow the movements involved in breathing. As you inhale, see if you can sense the downward movement of the air and your diaphragm. See if your belly expands as you inhale. If not, gently put your palms over your navel, and sense how the warmth from your palms begins to attract your breath and open your belly. As you exhale, see if you can sense the upward movement of the diaphragm and the inward movement of your belly. As you continue following these movements, notice how far they reach in your body. As you inhale, for example, see how far down the movement actually goes. Does the movement reach your pelvic floor? As you exhale, see how far up the movement goes. Does it reach your head? Don't try to "do" anything. Simply watch as your breath begins to take in more of your body. Work in this way for 10 minutes or so.

2 Sensing the inner movements of breath

As you continue to sense these upward and downward movements in the tissues of your body, include the movements of your "breath energy." As you inhale, see if you can sense some kind of energy, of vibration, rising upward into your head. As you exhale, see if you can sense this vibration moving downward through your whole body. Give yourself plenty of time. Using our inner attention to follow these movements is not something we are accustomed to doing. The key is to let go of any unnecessary tension and just keep "listening" to your sensation.

3 Making contact with your head and feet

Next, sense your feet resting firmly on the floor. Allow them to relax, as though they were spreading out over and even down into the floor. As they relax, you may begin to feel a vibration at the point in your foot called "bubbling springs" (the Kidney 1 acupuncture point at the upper part of the middle of your foot, as shown in Figure 24). Allow that vibration to spread into your whole foot, and even upward into your leg. Then, for a minute or two, massage the crown point at the top of your head with your index and middle fingers (Figure 25). Rest and sense the point opening. You may feel this opening as a subtle vibration, a melting, a prickly sensation, or a kind of numbness. In any event, keep your attention there until you experience a sensation of some kind.

4 Sensing your whole body breathing

As you keep your attention on your feet and crown you will begin to sense your whole body involved in breathing. As you inhale, you may feel as though you are drawing the bubbling sensation in your feet all the way up through the tissues and organs of your body to join with the breath energy moving to the top of your head. As you exhale, you may sense the inner energy of your breath spreading downward through your entire body toward your feet. When this happens, just enjoy this sensation of the breath energy moving upward and downward in your

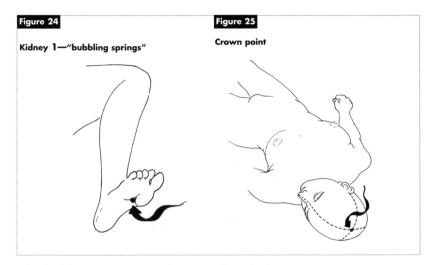

Figure 24

Kidney 1—"bubbling springs"

Figure 25

Crown point

body. Observe any areas where your breath does not seem to penetrate or move. Work for at least 10 minutes in this way, simply observing the rising and falling of energy, of sensation, through your body. If you don't feel these movements yet, don't worry. This can take time. Just go on to the next practice.

5 Lengthening your spine

Stand again in the basic standing posture, with your knees slightly bent and your feet parallel, about shoulder width apart. Let your shoulders relax and your arms simply hang at your sides. Put your attention on the bubbling springs point on both feet and on the crown point. Feel the vibration in both areas. Allow your inhalation to rise from your feet and go all the way up to and out through the top of your head. As it moves up through the top of your spine and your head you may, especially during your first few breaths, sense your spine being lengthened and your head being pulled upward so that it rests more lightly on your spine. Allow your exhalation to start from the top of your head and go down through your feet into the earth. Be sure to stay in touch with your spine as you exhale; see if you can maintain its length. Feel as though your breath is simultaneously raising you upward and rooting

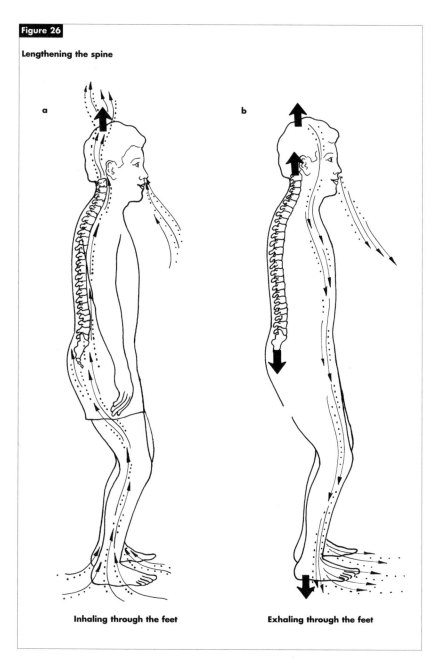

Figure 26

Lengthening the spine

a

b

Inhaling through the feet

Exhaling through the feet

you downward (Figure 26). Don't think about the irrationality of this experience—just let it happen.

6 Connecting heaven and earth

Once you've been able to sense these movements, try the following exercise using the same basic standing position. As you inhale, slowly rise up on your toes, and simultaneously raise your arms up in front of you. Your arms should arrive straight over your head (palms facing forward) at the same time that you have reached your full extension (Figure 27). As you exhale, slowly lower your arms and feet until you are in the original standing position. Try this many times. Sense the upward and downward movement of energy. Sense your whole body breathing. Experience how your breath is putting you in touch with your own verticality—connecting heaven and earth both inside and outside your body. Once you've felt this, walk around for a few minutes and see how long you can maintain this sensation.

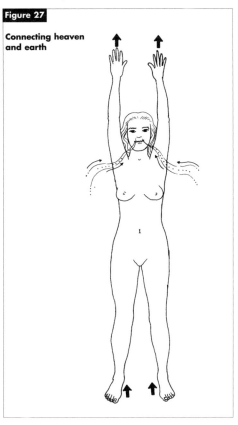

Figure 27

Connecting heaven and earth

THE SPACIOUS  BREATH

… each breath we take is filled
not only with the nutrients and energies
we need for life, but also with the expansive,
open quality of space. It is this quality
of spaciousness, if we allow it to enter us,
that can help us open to deeper levels
of our own being and to our own
inner powers of healing.

Thirty spokes together make a wheel for a cart.
    It is the empty space in the center
of the wheel which enables it to be used.
Mold clay into a vessel;
it is the emptiness within
that creates the usefulness of the vessel.
Cut out doors and windows in a house;
it is the empty space inside
that creates the usefulness of the house.
Thus, what we have may be something substantial,
But its usefulness lies in the unoccupied, empty space.
The substance of your body is enlivened
by maintaining the part of you that is unoccupied.[39]

                                        Lao Tzu

To experience the natural healing power of breath is to experience its inherent "spaciousness." Our breath can not only move upward and downward to help us experience our own verticality, but it can also move inward and outward to expand and connect our inner spaces with the space of the so-called outer world. In the same way that our experience of external space allows us to differentiate and relate to each other and the various objects and processes of the outer world, our experience of the internal spaces, the "chambers" of our bodies and psyches, allows us to differentiate the various functions and energies of our organism and keep them in dynamic harmony. As Chuang Tzu states:

"All things that have consciousness depend upon breath. But if they do not get their fill of breath, it is not the fault of Heaven. Heaven opens up the passages and supplies them day and night without stop. But man on the contrary blocks up the holes. The cavity of the body is a many-storied vault; the mind has its heavenly wanderings. But if the chambers are not large and roomy, then the wives and sisters will fall to quarreling. If the mind does not have its heavenly wanderings, then the six apertures of sensation will defeat each other."[40]

Clearly, for Chuang Tzu and the Taoists, the various chambers or stories of the human organism—especially the abdomen, chest, and head—need to be experienced as "large and roomy" if our various functions and energies are to work in full harmony. Without some sense of spaciousness in our organs and tissues, we are unable to feel space in the other aspects of our lives. It is just this feeling that there is no space in our lives, that there is no room to expand our experience of ourselves, that lies at the root of much of our stress and dis-ease. It is one of the main reasons we so cherish trips to the countryside or ocean, where we find not only expansive vistas of land and sky, but also profound, inexhaustible silence. Though these spacious experiences of our eyes and ears help open up our psychological structure, including our feelings and mind, the sense of spaciousness and silence quickly disappears when we return to our ordinary circumstances.

The Tibetan Buddhists also put great emphasis on the importance of space to our well-being, making clear that the "feeling of lack of space, whether on a personal, psychological level or an interpersonal, sociological level, has led to experience of confusion, conflict, imbalance, and general negativity within modern society.... But if we can begin to open our perspective and discover new dimensions of space within our immediate experiences, the anxiety and frustration which results from our sense of limitation will automatically be lessened; and we can increase our ability to relate sensitively and effectively to ourselves, to others, and to our environment."[41]

LEVELS OF SENSATION

The discovery of "new dimensions of space within our immediate experiences" lies at the foundation of health and inner growth. Because our most immediate experience is the sensation of our own body, it is here that we can most effectively begin this discovery. The sensation of the body can be experienced at many different levels, and it is just this organic experience of various levels, of various densities of sensation, that begins to give us a taste of internal spaciousness. These levels include the sensation of superficial aches and pains; the compact sensation of the weight and form of the body; the more subtle sensation of temperature, movement, and touch; the tingling sensation of the totality of the skin; the living, breathing sensation of the inner structure of the fascia, the muscles, the organs, the fluids, and the bones; and the integrative, vibratory sensation of the body's energy centers and pathways.

But there is one more level of sensation that we are given as our birthright. This is the all-encompassing sensation of openness that lies at the heart of being. As our sensation begins to open up, as we sense a broader frequency of vibration in our experience of ourselves (a vibration that *includes* instead of excluding), we come into touch with the sensation of the energy of life itself—before it is conditioned by the rigid mental, emotional, and physical forms of the society in which we live, and, even more importantly, by our own self-image. As we learn more and more about how to allow this direct sensation of life into our experience of ourselves, we feel a growing spaciousness, a sense of wonder in which the restrictions of our self-image can begin to dissolve. It is the organic experience of this essential spaciousness that embraces the various polarities and contradictions of our lives, the various manifestations of yin and yang, and allows them to exist side by side in our being without reaction. This inner, organic embrace, this sensory acceptance of everything that we are, frees not only our body but also our mind and feelings, bringing us a new sense of vitality and wholeness.

THE THREE BREATHING SPACES

To experience this inner, organic embrace, however, requires that we begin to open up the various chambers of our being, allowing them to return to their original "large and roomy" condition. The most direct way to begin this process is to learn how to experience the essential spaciousness of our breath and to guide this spaciousness consciously into ourselves—into what Ilse Middendorf calls our "three breathing spaces." These spaces are the lower breathing space, from the navel downward; the middle space from the navel to the diaphragm; and the upper space from the diaphragm up through the head (Figure 28). By learning how to breathe into and experience these spaces, we begin to open to ourselves in new ways. We learn how to relax all unnecessary tension and to find dynamic relaxation, the ideal balance between tension and relaxation, in our own tissues—in the various boundaries of these spaces. And this work, in itself, can bring about many important changes both in our perception of ourselves and in our health.

The idea of the three breathing spaces coincides from an anatomical standpoint almost exactly with the concept of the "triple burner," or "triple warmer," in Chinese medicine. The triple burner is one of the basic systems of the body, a system with a name and a function but no specific form. It consists of an upper, middle, and lower energetic space, each of which contains within it various organs. From the standpoint of Chinese medicine, the triple burner integrates, harmonizes, and regulates the metabolic and physiologic processes of the primary organ networks. It is associated with the overall movement of chi and is also responsible for communication among the various organs of the body. It is my experience that consciously bringing the breath into

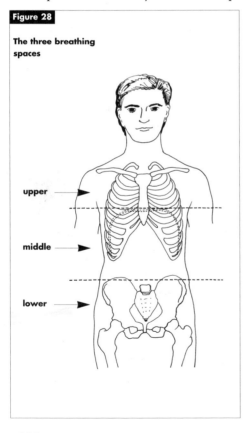

Figure 28

The three breathing spaces

upper

middle

lower

each breathing space, into each burner, and sensing the spacious movement of the breath up and down through the spaces and the organs within these spaces, has a powerful balancing effect on my physical and psychological energies. If I work with this practice before I go to bed at night, it calms me and helps me sleep better; if I work with it during the day, it brings me a sense of greater relaxed vitality.

This work with the breathing spaces of the body is extremely powerful. In writing about the results of her approach to the breath through working with the various breathing spaces of the body, for example, Middendorf points out that "Through practicing and working on the breath we constantly create and experience new breathing spaces. This enables the body to free itself from its dullness and lack of liveliness, so that it feels easy and light through the continuing breathing movement and filled with new power, it feels good and more capable. This dynamic way of breathing can lead to great achievement and success in every expression of life. With its healing power it also reaches symptoms, states of exhaustion, depressions. An increasing ability to breathe will prevent these states from occurring anymore."[42]

Whatever theoretical framework we may choose for understanding our work with breath, each breath we take is filled not only with the nutrients and energies we need for life, but also with the expansive, open quality of space. It is this quality of spaciousness, if we allow it to enter us, that can help us open to deeper levels of our own being and to our own inner powers of healing. In spite of its simplicity, however, spacious breathing is not an easy practice to learn. Years of conditioning and "ignor-ance" have left us not only with many bad breathing habits, but, perhaps even more importantly, with little kinesthetic awareness of our own physical structure, and with how this structure hinders or supports our breathing. Without this inner sensation of our structure, any attempt to impose a new way of breathing—whether yogic, Taoist, or any other form—on our organism can only lead to confusion, and, potentially, further problems.

PSYCHOLOGICAL OBSTACLES TO AUTHENTIC BREATHING

Once we begin to get in touch with the sensation of this structure, however, we will begin to become aware of the mental and emotional forces acting on our breath, on our own particular rhythms of inhalation and exhalation. This is a crucial aspect of any serious work with breathing, since it will show us the psychological obstacles to discovering our own authentic breath.

Our Inability to Exhale Fully

According to Magda Proskauer, a psychiatrist and pioneer in breath therapy, one of the main obstacles "to discovering one's genuine breathing pattern" is the inability that many of us have to exhale fully. Whereas inhalation requires a certain amount of tension, exhalation requires letting go of this tension. Full inhalation without full exhalation is impossible. It is important, therefore, to see what stands in the way of full exhalation. For many of us, what stands in the way is often what is no longer necessary in our lives. Proskauer points out that "Our incapacity to exhale naturally seems to parallel the psychological condition in which we are often filled with old concepts and long-since-consumed ideas, which, just like the air in our lungs, are stale and no longer of any use."[43] She makes it clear that in order to exhale fully we need to learn how to let go "of our burdens, of our cross which we carry on our shoulders." By letting go of this unnecessary weight, we allow our shoulders and ribs to relax, to sink downward into their natural position instead of tensing upward. Full exhalation follows quite naturally.

Our Inability to Inhale Fully

Those of us who are unable to exhale fully in the normal circumstances of our lives are obviously unable to inhale fully as well. In full inhalation, which originates in the lower breathing space and moves gradually upward through the other spaces, one's abdomen, lower back, and rib cage must all expand. This, as we have seen in earlier chapters, helps the diaphragm, which is attached all around the bottom of the rib cage and anchored to the spine in the lumbar area, to achieve its full range of movement downward. For this to happen, the muscles and organs involved in breathing must be in a state of dynamic harmony, free from unnecessary tension. But this expansion is not just a physical phenomenon, it is also a psychological one. It depends on both the wish and the ability to engage fully with our lives, to take in new impressions of ourselves and the world.

Freedom To Embrace the Unknown

Full exhalation and inhalation are thus most possible when we are free enough to let go of the known and embrace the unknown. In full exhalation, we empty ourselves—not just of carbon dioxide, but also of old tensions, concepts, and feelings. In full inhalation, we renew ourselves—not just with new oxygen, but also with new impressions of everything in and around us. Both movements of our breath depend on the "unoccupied, empty space" that lies at the center of our being. It is the sensation of this inner space (and silence)—which we can sometimes experience in the natural pause between exhalation and inhalation—that is our path into the unknown. It is the sensation of this space that can enliven us and make us whole.

PRACTICE

To prepare for this practice, sit or stand quietly with your eyes open and experience the coming and going of your breath. Get in touch with the three tan tiens—just below the navel, in the solar plexus, and between the eyebrows. Sense the different qualities of vibration in these areas. As you breathe, sense your outer and inner breath—the various upward and downward movements of both tissue and energy. Clearly note any areas that seem to be tense or closed to your breath. Spend at least 10 minutes on this stage of the practice.

1 Opening your breathing spaces

During exhalation, use two or three fingers to press gently into your lower abdomen, between your pubic bone and your navel. During inhalation, gradually release the pressure. Sense how your abdomen responds to this pressure. Take several breaths this way. Now put your hands over your navel, and work in the same way—pressing as you exhale, and gradually releasing the pressure as you inhale. Notice how your lower breathing space begins to open.

Next, put your hands over your lower ribs on both sides of your trunk. As you exhale, gently press your ribs inward with your hands. As you inhale, gradually release the pressure from your hands and sense your ribs expanding outward. It is helpful to realize that the lower ribs, also called the "floating ribs," can expand quite freely since they are not attached to your sternum. In fact, the expansion of the floating ribs helps create more space for the lungs to expand at their widest point.

Now, apply light pressure to your solar plexus as you exhale. Again, watch for several minutes as your upper abdomen begins to relax and open. Next, as you exhale, press lightly on the bottom of your sternum. Taking several breaths in each position, gradually work your way up toward the top of the sternum. If you take your time and work gently, you will find your various breathing spaces beginning to become more elastic and spacious. Now try this same approach with any areas of your abdomen, rib cage (both on and between your ribs), shoulders, and so on that seem overly tight or constricted. Take your time. It is actually better to do this work for 15 or 20 minutes each day over a period of a week or so than to try to do it all in one session.

2 A simple technique for opening the three breathing spaces

There is another, simple technique that you can experiment with to help open the three breathing spaces. This technique, which I learned several years ago from Ilse Middendorf, involves pressing the appropriate finger pads of one hand against those of the other. To help open the lower space, press the pads of the little fingers and the pads of the ring fingers together firmly but without force. For the middle space, press the pads of the middle fingers together. For the upper space, press the pads of the thumbs and index fingers

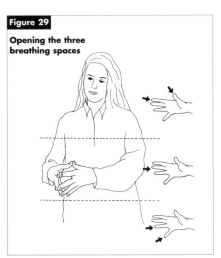

Figure 29

Opening the three breathing spaces

together. To help open all the spaces simultaneously, press the pads of all five fingers together (Figure 29). When you first begin this practice do not take more than take eight breaths while pressing your finger pads together.

3 Movement of spaciousness

Once you feel more of the whole of yourself involved in breathing, put most of your attention on the movement of air through your nose during inhalation. Take several long, slow breaths. Feel the empty, expansive, spacious quality of the air as it moves down through your trachea and into your lungs. But don't stop there. As you continue your inhalation, sense this spaciousness moving downward through all the tissues and organs of your abdomen and filling your entire lower breathing space. Allow this feeling of space to release any tensions and absorb any stagnant energies residing below your navel. As you exhale slowly, use your attention to direct these tensions and energies out with your breath. Then work in the same way with the middle breathing space (from the navel to the diaphragm) and with the upper breathing space (from the diaphragm to the top of the head), sensing the various tissues and organs inside these spaces. When you have worked with all three breathing spaces, stop working intentionally with the feeling of space and simply follow your breathing.

4 Sensing the breath of the spine

Now that you have some direct awareness of the three major breathing spaces, especially in relation to the front of the body, we're going to work with the inner space of the spine, the very core of our body, which connects the three breathing spaces in the back. In particular, we're going to sense the craniosacral rhythm of the cerebrospinal fluid as it pulses through the central canal of the spine, moving from the brain down to the sacrum. The cerebrospinal fluid—a clear fluid produced from red blood flowing through a rich supply of blood vessels deep within the brain—not only provides nutrients for the brain and spine, but also removes the toxic products of metabolism and functions as a shock absorber. The pressure of this fluid has an influence on nerve flow and affects the ability of the senses and brain to take in new impressions.

Lie down on your back with your legs stretched out and your arms at your side. Sense again the expansion and contraction of your breath as it moves through the three breathing spaces, the three burners. See if you can include your heartbeat in your sensation. After several minutes, put your fingers on your temples above your ears (you can rest your elbows on the ground) and sense the pulse of your heartbeat in your temples. Sense the way your head expands on inhalation and contracts on exhalation. You may also begin to feel the way your whole body takes part in this ongoing rhythm of expansion and contraction.

After two or three minutes working in this way, hold your breath intentionally after inhaling. See if you can sense an inner expansion and contraction radiating from the area of the head and spine. Make sure that you don't hold your breath for any longer than is comfortable. After taking several more spontaneous breaths, again hold your breath and touch the tip of your tongue to the center of the roof of your mouth. Later in the book we will go into the significance of this in completing the circuit of energy flow called the microcosmic orbit, but for now just see if you can sense the roof of your mouth expanding and contracting in rhythm with your head and spine. If so, what you are sensing is the pulsation of your cerebrospinal fluid. An entire cycle of expansion and contraction can take from five to eight seconds.

5 Sense your spine and breathing spaces at the same time

Now without losing touch with the "breathing" of your spine, include the three breathing spaces in your sensation of yourself. As you sense the pulsation of your spine, also sense the three breathing spaces as they empty and fill. As you exhale, the spaces contract from top to bottom. As you inhale, the spaces expand from bottom to top. *Don't force anything.* Just let yourself experience the process of natural breathing— a process in which the various spaces of your body all participate. Feel how with each breath the spaces are becoming "large and roomy." Let your awareness enter these spaces and enjoy the comfort of this natural process of expansion and contraction. After several minutes, get up and either sit cross-legged or on a chair. Continue to work with spacious breathing for several more minutes, noticing any changes brought about by your new posture.

6 The pause of spaciousness

Now simply follow your breathing. Notice the two pauses in your breathing cycle: one after inhalation and one after exhalation. Pay particular attention to the pause after exhalation. The great mystical traditions have spoken of this pause between exhalation and inhalation as a timeless moment—an infinite space—between yin and yang, nonaction and action, in which we can go beyond our self-image and experience our own unconditioned nature. See if you can at least sense this pause as an entranceway into yourself—into the healing spaciousness of your own deepest sensation of yourself. Don't try to force anything. Just watch and sense. Work like this for at least 10 minutes.

7 Spacious breathing under stress

It is relatively easy to have the sense of spaciousness when we are in quiet, undemanding circumstances. And it is important, especially at the beginning, to practice this kind of breathing in such circumstances. Eventually, however, you will want to begin to try spacious breathing, especially into your navel area, in the often stress-filled circumstances of your everyday life. For it is here that you will, with practice, have the largest impact on your overall well-being and health, and it is here that you will gain important new insights into your own nature. What's more, it is here that you will have an opportunity to discover a deep inner sensation of yourself that is somehow "separate" from the automatic reactions of your sympathetic nervous system (your "fight or flight" reflex), an overall sensation of yourself that will, if you can stay in touch with it, dissolve any unnecessary tension and bring about the appropriate degree of relaxation to meet the real demands of the moment.

To help prepare for working in such conditions, try the following practice. Stand with your weight balanced equally on both feet and your knees slightly bent. Sense the whole of yourself standing there, breathing. Let the sensation of yourself go deeper and deeper with each breath. Without losing this overall sensation of yourself, let your weight shift to your right foot. Bring your left foot up along the inner side of your right leg all the way up to your groin. Use your hands to help you position the heel of your foot in the area of your groin with your toes pointed upward if possible. Now raise your arms up from your sides (palms facing up) until your palms meet over your head (Figure 30). If this posture is too easy for you, if it does not arouse any stress, you might try closing your eyes and moving your arms up and down as you stand on one leg. If your health will not permit you to stand on one leg or to raise your arms above your head, then be inventive—find other ways to make the posture challenging for yourself.

Now, staying in this posture, let your chest and belly relax, and then begin to breathe into your lower abdomen. As you inhale, sense the spaciousness filling your lower abdomen; as you exhale, sense all your tensions going out with your breath. Breathe in this way for two or three minutes; then put your tongue to the roof of your mouth and see if you can also sense the pulsation of the cerebrospinal fluid. When you finish, slowly return your arms to your sides with your palms facing down and return to the original standing position with both feet on the ground. Sense your whole body breathing. Can you notice any differences between the left and right sides? Reverse your legs and repeat the entire process.

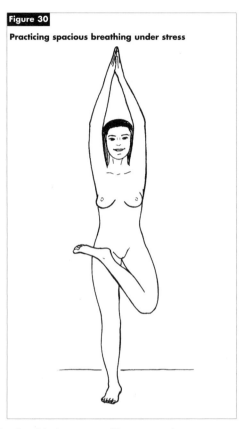

Figure 30

Practicing spacious breathing under stress

Because it is relatively difficult, this is an excellent exercise to prepare you to practice spacious breathing in the midst of tension and stress. The key is to learn how to relax inside this difficult posture. If you find that your belly and chest stay tense, put your attention on your face, ears, and tongue, and just let them relax. Because your face most directly reflects the tensions of your self-image, it is by learning how to relax your face that you can begin to relax the rest of your body. Try breathing directly into your entire face, especially in the area of the upper tan tien. Let space permeate your nose, eyes, ears, and so on. Then return to breathing in your lower abdomen.

If you begin to lose your balance at any time during this exercise, don't resist, don't try to compete with gravity. Whatever happens, stay in touch with the whole sensation of yourself, including your awkwardness (your body knows how to take care of itself without the help of your self-image). If you do fall, simply try again from the beginning. As you continue working in this way—not letting yourself react in the usual way to the difficulty of the posture or to your own awkwardness— you will begin to understand that this inner sensation of yourself is intimately related to a new, more inclusive level of awareness, a level of awareness that can transform your life.

8 Spacious breathing in the ordinary conditions of life

Once you are able to keep your belly, chest, and face relaxed during the previous practice, you are ready to try spacious breathing in the ordinary conditions of your life. Whatever you do, don't choose situations, especially at the beginning, that are so stressful that you will be doomed to failure. Start, rather, with ordinary situations—walking down the street, talking to a friend, and so on. Then, as you get a better feel of the practice in these conditions, you can move on to those that are more difficult. Eventually you will want to try spacious breathing when you are tense or emotional. Try it, for example, when you are in the middle of an argument with someone, or when you are lost in self-pity, anger, worry, impatience, and so on. If you are able to remember to practice in these more difficult conditions, you will experience first-hand how spacious breathing can help transform the stress and negativity that is bound up with your self-image into the energy you need for your own vitality and well-being.

As you undertake these practices, try them in a light, playful, and experimental way—from the standpoint of learning firsthand about yourself. As you continue this "playful" work with spacious breathing over many weeks and months, you will notice various tensions beginning to dissolve as if on their own. You will also notice your breath occupying more of each breathing space. These changes will make it possible for you to observe deep-rooted patterns of tension in the various postures and movements of your organism, patterns that inhibit the sensation of energy and movement and stand in the way of your becoming more available to the whole of yourself. You will also begin to sense that these patterns are related to, or even fueled by, various old attitudes and ideas, as well as chronic negative emotions, that create and maintain your self-image and leave little space for new experiences and perceptions. You may also observe that it is just these attitudes, ideas, and emotions that are the main obstacles to natural breathing and thus to your health and well-being.

to help draw energy deep into their tissues and bones, as well as to direct energy—for storage, for action, or for healing—to any part of their organism. It is also used to build up what is called "guardian chi," a protective shield of energy around the body that helps ward off negative influences, including bacteria and viruses dangerous to our health. It is thus especially useful to help immune system functioning.

Part of the reason for the great power of this practice is the change in the pressure differential between the chest and abdomen. When the diaphragm moves downward and the belly contracts inward during inhalation, the resulting pressure in the abdomen helps "pack" the breath energy into the abdominal tissues and organs, as well as into the spine. When the diaphragm relaxes upward and the belly relaxes outward during exhalation, the sudden release of pressure guides the energy outward wherever one's attention is directed. It is therefore extremely important when undertaking reverse breathing to be clear about where one puts one's attention. Otherwise one's energy may be quickly lost.

In spite of its many benefits, reverse breathing should only be undertaken when one is quite comfortable with natural abdominal breathing. Without this level of comfort, most people who attempt reverse breathing tense their faces, necks, and chests and draw their diaphragms upward as they inhale. This not only negates the positive effects of the practice, but can also lead to a variety of problems, including chest pain, diarrhea, an increase in heartbeat or blood pressure, and energy stagnation. It can also lead to mental and emotional confusion and a scattering of the energy of awareness.

PRACTICE

Though you can practice reverse breathing in a sitting posture, it is best, especially at the beginning, to use a standing posture. This will make it easier to feel your weight sinking and thus will help counteract any tendency to pull your diaphragm upward as you inhale. To prepare for this practice, do tan tien breathing for several minutes, making sure that your shoulders and chest stay relaxed. Also check to make sure that your diaphragm moves downward as you inhale and upward as you exhale. Breathe in this way until you begin to feel a definite warmth or vibration in your belly.

1 Reverse the breathing process

When you feel this warmth, draw your belly slowly back toward your spine as you inhale, and let it relax outward as you exhale. As you inhale, be sure to keep your chest relaxed and to sense your diaphragm moving downward. As it does so, you will feel pressure building up in your lower abdomen, even all the way down to your perineum. If you sense any pressure in your solar plexus area, you need to relax your chest more and to be sure that your diaphragm is moving downward as you inhale. One way to support this relaxation is to let your shoulders move slightly forward and to sense your sternum shifting slightly downward.

2 Guide the energy to specific areas

As reverse breathing begins to become more natural to you, start paying more attention to the quality of the energy being packed into your abdomen as you inhale. As you exhale, allow this energy to expand outward to nourish your entire body. You can also use your attention to help guide this energy to any particular part of your body that you wish to help heal. If you're having a problem in a particular area, continue to inhale into your abdomen, but visualize and sense your breath energy going to the problem area as you exhale.

The Psychological Dimensions of the Microcosmic Orbit

According to Taoist master Mantak Chia, each of the energy centers of the microcosmic orbit influences our emotions in a particular way, depending on the degree to which the center is opened or closed. In my own personal work with the microcosmic orbit, it has become quite clear to me that learning how to sense these various centers, or points, helps open them so that energy can flow more freely throughout the organism. This work with sensation is also a direct path to self-knowledge.

The following outline of the energy centers and their emotional influences (derived mainly from Mantak Chia's teachings and books) is not meant to be exhaustive or final. As you begin to learn how to use your breath to sense your body and emotions in the midst of the daily activities of your life, you may find psychological traits other than those listed associated with these centers. What is certain is that working in this way will bring you to a new understanding of yourself, particularly of the relationship between your physical life and your psychological life.

Navel Center

Taoist sages and Chinese medical practitioners regard the navel center, which includes the lower tan tien, not only as the physical center of the body, but also as the body's main "storage battery" for chi. As Mantak Chia states: "The navel center was our first connection with the outside world. All oxygen, blood, and nutrients flowed into our fetal forms through this abdominal doorway. As a result, the navel center has a special sensitivity that continues far beyond the cutting of the umbilical cord at birth; it stays with us throughout our entire lives."[61]

Closed: One experiences a lack of psychological balance—a sense of being distracted or critical. One is not open to receive new impressions.

Opened: One feels a sensation of openness to the world, a sensation of being centered.

Sexual Center

This center—located for women slightly above the pubic bone and between the ovaries, and for men at the base of the penis about one and one-half inches inside the body—is the basic energy "generator" in the human body.

Closed: One feels an overall lack of energy and little enjoyment from life. One feels self-destructive, negative, and listless.

Opened: One feels a sense of personal, creative power, and the ability to get things done.

Perineum

The perineum is located between the sexual organs and anus. Because of its anatomical position, it connects the two channels of the microcosmic orbit and serves as the foundation for the inner organs of the abdomen.

Closed: One feels insecure and lonely. One also fears any kind of change.

Opened: One feels grounded, rooted to the earth and its healing energies. One also feels a sense of peacefulness.

Sacrum and Coccyx

Though the coccyx and sacrum represent two different locations, we will treat them as one for the purposes of the microcosmic orbit. It is in the sacrum and coccyx that many major nerves from the organs and glands come together, and energy is directed up the spine. It is in this area that the Taoists believe that earth energy and sexual energy are refined and transformed before they move up to the higher centers.

Closed: One feels unbalanced, heavy, and hopeless. One feels that the past is a prison, and that one is under the sway of many unconscious fears.

Opened: One feels light and balanced. One feels that the past is a resource that can be drawn upon for a deeper understanding of and engagement with life.

Kidney Center

The kidney center is located between the second and third lumbar vertebrae of the spine. You can find this point by putting your finger on your spine opposite the navel, and then bending forward at this point. The vertebra that protrudes the most marks the area of the kidney center. Called the door of life, or the mingmen, this center is where our prenatal vitality, our sexual essence, is stored.

Closed: One feels fear and a lack of balance. One also feels a lack of vital energy.
Opened: One experiences feelings of openness, abundance, and generosity.

Adrenal Center

The adrenal center (T11), located between the eleventh and twelfth thoracic vertebrae opposite the solar plexus, lies between the two adrenal glands which sit on top of the kidneys. The adrenal glands, which produce adrenaline and noradrenaline as well as a variety of other hormones, are the primary energy source for the sympathetic nervous system, and are activated whenever there is stress and the instinctive "fight or flight" response.

Closed: One feels either hyper or listless. Old fears can return and begin to shape our experience and behavior.
Opened: One feels a sense of vitality and confidence.

Center Opposite the Heart

This center, which is located between the fifth and sixth thoracic vertebrae between the shoulder blades, has a close relationship with the functioning of the heart and thymus gland.

Closed: One feels a sense of burden and hopelessness. One also feels a sense of chaos.
Opened: One has a feeling of freedom, as well as a deep-felt sense of living.

Center Opposite the Throat

This center, located just below the seventh cervical vertebra (C7), is the central junction box where the energies, nerves, and tendons from the upper and lower parts of the body meet. Any blockage of this center restricts the flow of energy up the spine to the higher centers in the head. You can easily find this point by bending your head forward; the vertebra that protrudes the most is C7.

Closed: One feels disconnected from both oneself and others. One feels a sense of stubbornness and inappropriateness.
Opened: One feels able to embrace both oneself and others with humanity.

Small Brain Center

Sometimes called the jade pillow, this center lies above the first cervical vertebra in the hollow at the base of the skull. This center includes the cerebellum and medulla oblongata, which help control muscle coordination, as well as respiration and heartbeat. For the Taoist, this center is a storage place for the earth force and for refined sexual energy.

Closed: One feels dullness, burden, and suffocation. One may also experience neck pain.
Opened: One feels inspired.

Crown Center

This center is at the top of the head, where an imaginary line from the top of one ear to the top of the other intersects with the midline of the head. This center has a special relationship with the pineal gland, as well as with the thalamus and the hypothalamus. The crown center is connected with the central nervous system, as well as with the sensory/motor system.

Closed: One may fall under the influence of illusions or delusions, losing oneself either in a false sense of pride or the feeling of being a victim. One may have erratic mood swings and headaches.
Opened: One radiates a deep happiness, and feels that one is receiving guidance from higher forces.

Pituitary Center

This center, sometimes called the third eye, lies midway between the eyebrows approximately three inches inside the skull. This center produces hormones that govern a wide range of bodily functions. The Taoists believe that this center is the home of the spirit.

Closed: One feels a lack of aim, of decisiveness. The mind wanders and is unable to make decisions.

Opened: One feels a sense of real purpose, as well as a sense of direct knowing, of intuition.

Throat Center

This center, which includes the thyroid and parathyroid glands, is located in the V-like space at the bottom of the throat just above the sternum. The functions of this center include speech, dreaming, the production of growth hormones, and the regulation of the metabolism.

Closed: One feels choked up and unwilling or unable to communicate or to change.

Opened: One is able to communicate clearly, even eloquently, and one's dreams are more lucid.

Heart Center

From an energetic standpoint, the heart center is between the nipples in men, and approximately one inch up from the bottom of the sternum in women. The opening to the heart center is very small, so this center can be easily blocked or congested. The heart center governs not only the heart but also the thymus gland, which is an important part of our immunological system.

Closed: One feels any one of a variety of negative emotions, including arrogance, self-pity, impatience, and hatred.

Opened: One feels joy, love, patience, honesty, and respect for oneself and others.

Solar Plexus Center

This center is about three-quarters of the way up between the navel and the bottom of the sternum. This center is related to several organs, including the stomach, spleen, pancreas, and liver. It is in the cauldron of the solar plexus that Taoists believe that the sexual energy (ching) and life-force energy (chi) are transformed into spiritual energy (shen). Mantak Chia believes that although it is important for the solar plexus center to be opened, "if it is too open, one may be overly sensitive to the thoughts, feelings, and opinions of others, to the point of being unable to shut off mental and emotional static when in the company of others."[62]

Closed: One feels panic and worry. One is overly cautious.

Opened: One feels a sense of inner freedom, and the ability to take risks on behalf of oneself or others.

NOTES

1   P. D. Ouspensky, *In Search of the Miraculous* (New York: Harcourt, Brace & World, 1949), p. 387.

2   Karlfried Durckheim, *Hara: The Vital Center of Man* (London: George Allen & Unwin, 1970), pp. 154-55.

3   Of course, hyperventilation can be a powerful tool in the work of transformation. On pages 170-184 of Stanislov Grof's book *The Adventure of Self-Discovery* (New York: State University of New York Press, 1988), the author, a well-known psychiatrist and founder of "holotropic therapy," points out that sustained hyperventilation helps to loosen psychological defenses and bring about a "profound emotional release and physical relaxation." Grof believes that this occurs not just through the traditional psychiatric mechanism of catharsis, but also because hyperventilation brings to the surface "deep tensions" in the form of "lasting contractions and prolonged spasms ... that consume enormous amounts of pent-up energy." In Grof's framework, it is the eventual burning up of this energy through these sustained contractions and spasms that brings about psychophysical transformation. This is usually intensely emotional work, and the person undertaking it may require a great deal of individual therapeutic attention. What's more, according to Grof, since hyperventilation initially amplifies and makes manifest the various psychophysical tensions in the organism, it is important to continue this form of breathing until resolution and release take place. As fascinating and important as Grof's work is, it is my intent in this book to show how it is possible to rediscover our natural, authentic breath in the ordinary conditions of life, without the need for psychiatric help. I will not, therefore, explore the therapeutic techniques of hyperventilation any further.

4   See, for example, *The Jade Emperor's Mind Seal Classic: A Taoist Guide to*

Health, Longevity and Immortality, trans. Stuart Alve Olson (St. Paul: Dragon Door Publications, 1992), pp. 69-71.

5 Lao Tzu, *The Complete Works of Lao Tzu,* trans. Ni, Hua-Ching (Santa Monica, Calif.: Seven Star Communications, 1989), p. 14.

6 This "ultradian" rhythm, long observed by medical science, is related to the functioning of the brain hemispheres and can play an important role in healing. When the left nostril is more open, the right hemisphere of the brain is generally more dominant; when the right nostril is more open, the left hemisphere is generally more dominant. One can intentionally open a nostril that is more congested and thus make the other hemisphere more active by lying down on one's side with the congested nostril above and continuing to breathe through the nose. If one is feeling out of sorts or has a headache, trying this experiment for 15 or 20 minutes can often bring relief.

7 Swami Rama, Rudolph Ballentine, and Alan Hymes, *Science of Breath: A Practical Guide* (Honesdale, Pa.: Himalayan Institute, 1979), p. 41.

8 It is interesting to note that some diseases, such as diabetes, can increase the acidity of the blood without increasing carbon dioxide. Since the respiratory center is unable to differentiate the cause of this increase in acidity, it automatically increases the breath rate.

9 Even people with severe pulmonary problems can quickly benefit from work with breathing. In experiments at Shanghai No. 2 Tuberculosis Hospital, 27 people with pulmonary emphysema were able to increase the average range of their diaphragmatic movement from 2.8 centimeters at the beginning of their treatment to 4.9 centimeters after a year of training—an increase in diaphragmatic movement of more than 57 percent. The results are reported in *300 Questions on Qigong Exercises* (Guangzhou, China: Guandong Science and Technology Press, 1994), p. 257.

10 Mantak Chia, private paper.

11 See, for example, Charles Brooks, *Sensory Awareness: The Rediscovery of Experiencing* (New York: Viking Press, 1974).

12 Ilse Middendorf, *The Perceptible Breath: A Breathing Science* (Paderborn, Germany: Junfermann-Verlag, 1990).

13 Rollo May, *Love and Will* (New York: Dell Publishing Company, 1974), p. 237.

14 See, for example, Royce Flippin, "Slow Down, You Breathe Too Fast," *American Health: Fitness of Body and Mind*, Vol. 11, No. 5 (June 1992).

15 For a further explanation of neuropeptides, see Candace Pert, "The Chemical Communicators," in Bill Moyers, *Healing and the Mind* (New York: Doubleday, 1993) pp. 177-94.

16 See, for example, Lawrence Steinman, "Autoimmune Disease," *Scientific American*, September 1993 (Special Issue on "Life, Death, and the Immune System").

17 Ernest Lawrence Rossi, *The Psychobiology of Mind-Body Healing* (New York: Norton, 1988), pp. 173-74.

18 Another effective way to turn on the parasympathetic nervous system is through special movement and awareness practices such as tai chi and chi kung. Among many other benefits, these practices can help release unnecessary tension in the back, especially in the spine, where the main neurons of the central nervous system reside. It is my experience that people with frequent lower back pain are often the same people who have trouble not only relaxing but even admitting that they need to relax. When carried out in the correct way, tai chi and chi kung increase relaxation not only by making the spine more flexible, but also through the deeper breathing that they promote.

19 For further information on the subject of anger, see David Sobel and

Robert Ornstein, "Defusing Anger and Hostility," *Mental Medicine Update: The Mind/Body Newsletter,* Vol. 4, No. 3 (1995).

20 Moshe Feldenkrais, *The Potent Self: A Guide to Spontaneity* (San Francisco: Harper & Row, 1985), p. 95.

21 Peter Nathan, *The Nervous System* (Oxford: Oxford University Press, 1982), p. 48.

22 See James Wyckoff, *Wilhelm Reich: Life Force Explorer* (Greenwich, Conn.: Fawcett Publications, 1973).

23 See Moyers's book, *Healing and the Mind,* particularly the interview with David Eisenberg on the subject of chi (p. 255).

24 Andre van Lysebeth, *Pranayama: The Yoga of Breathing* (London: Unwin Paperbacks, 1983), p. 28.

25 Robert Ornstein and David Sobel, *The Healing Brain: Breakthrough Discoveries About How the Brain Keeps Us Healthy* (New York: Simon and Schuster, 1987), p. 207.

26 For more information on ions, see Fred Soyka with Alan Edmonds, *The Ion Effect: How Air Electricity Rules Your Life and Health* (New York: Bantam Books, 1977).

27 See *The Primordial Breath,* Volume 2, trans. Jane Huang (Torrance, Calif.: Original Books, 1990), p. 13, for a clear description of this very esoteric practice. I will not go into this practice since it is extremely advanced and I have little experience with it. I will, however, discuss in later chapters an associated practice, introduced to me by Mantak Chia, of breathing into and swallowing the saliva.

28 Mantak Chia and Maneewan Chia, *Awaken Healing Light of the Tao* (Huntington, N.Y.: Healing Tao Books, 1993), p. 41.

29 *Awaken Healing Light,* pp. 41 ff.

30 *Awaken Healing Light,* pp. 185-86.

31 Lao Tzu, *Tao Te Ching,* trans. Victor H. Mair (New York: Bantam Books, 1990), p. 69.

32 Taoist reverse breathing often occurs spontaneously for anyone making great physical effort, especially in sports, martial arts, and so on, since it can help to generate outward force through the various limbs. To intentionally activate this form of breathing is quite difficult, however, and can, if done prematurely, cause a great deal of tension and have ill effects on the organism. Before trying reverse breathing it is best to have worked with abdominal breathing for at least several months.

33 Tzu Kuo Shih, *Qi Gong Therapy: The Chinese Art of Healing with Energy* (Barrytown, N.Y.: Station Hill Press, 1994), p. 35.

34 Robert B. Livingston, in *Gentle Bridges: Conversations with the Dalai Lama on the Sciences of the Mind,* eds. Jeremy W. Hayward and Francisco J. Varela (Boston: Shambhala, 1992), p. 174.

35 See pp. 47-54 of *Qi Gong Therapy* for a further discussion of some of the physiological results of respiratory exercises.

36 Chuang Tzu, *Basic Writings,* trans. Burton Watson (New York: Columbia University Press, 1964), p. 74.

37 Alexander Lowen, *The Spirituality of the Body: Bioenergetics for Grace and Harmony* (New York: Macmillan, 1990), pp. 37-38.

38 *Pranayama,* p. 31-32.

39 *The Complete Works of Lao Tzu,* p. 12.

40 *Basic Writings,* p. 138.

41 Tarthang Tulku, *Time, Space, and Knowledge: A New Vision of Reality* (Emeryville, Calif.: Dharma Publishing, 1977), p. 5.

42 *The Perceptible Breath,* p. 32.

43 From an article by Magda Proskauer, "The Therapeutic Value of Certain Breathing Techniques," in Charles Garfield, ed., *Rediscovery of the Body: A Psychosomatic View of Life and Death* (New York: A Laurel Original, 1977), pp. 59-60.

44 Recent biomedical research, such as that reported in Moyers's *Healing and the Mind,* makes it clear that what we think and feel can have an immediate positive or negative impact on our whole body, including our immune system. Of course, Taoism and other traditions have been aware of the influence of our thoughts and feelings on our health for thousands of years.

45 Norman Cousins, *Anatomy of an Illness* (New York: Bantam Books, 1979).

46 Mantak Chia, *Taoist Ways to Transform Stress into Vitality* (Huntington: N.Y.: Healing Tao Books, 1985), p. 33.

47 William James, *Psychology* (Greenwich, Conn.: Fawcett Publications, 1963), p. 335.

48 Moshe Feldenkrais, *The Elusive Obvious* (Cupertino, Calif.: Meta Publications, 1981), p. 61.

49 Paul Ekman and Richard J. Davidson, "Voluntary Smiling Changes Regional Brain Activity," *Psychological Science: A Journal of the American Psychological Society,* Vol. 4, No. 5 (September 1993), p. 345.

50 Phone conversation with Candace Pert, May 9, 1995 (see also note 15).

51 *Taoist Ways to Transform Stress*, p. 33.

52 For a contemporary, detailed description of scientific findings and Taoist beliefs regarding saliva, see the Winter 1993 issue of *The Healing Tao Journal*, Healing Tao Books, P.O. Box 1194, Huntington, NY 11743.

53 *In Search of the Miraculous*, p. 181.

54 *The Healing Brain*, p. 202.

55 From an article entitled "The Body's Guards" in *Living Right* (Winter 1995), p. 23.

56 Master Mantak Chia writes extensively about the microcosmic orbit in his 1993 book *Awaken Healing Light*, and offers readers many practical techniques for opening the governor and functional channels.

57 *Awaken Healing Light*, p. 170.

58 *Awaken Healing Light*, p. 496.

59 See Mantak Chia's book *Taoist Ways to Transform Stress* for the complete six healing sounds practice, including physical movements and postures.

60 My first experience with bellows breathing was highly instructive, since I had not yet understood how to breathe naturally. It took place during a spiritual retreat. On the first day, advanced breathing exercises were given to all of us, even beginners. To be sure, everyone at the retreat was told that these exercises should not be done from the ego or the will, but rather from a state of relaxation and exploration. But being instructed how to do something is not the same as being able to experience it. When we were asked, for example, to do bellows breathing (called *bastrika* in the various Indian traditions), the result for many people, including myself, was almost comical—frantic, spasmodic movements of various muscles all over the body, movements that seemed more willful than

skillful for most of us there. Even many of the more senior students had trouble carrying out the exercise in a harmonious way. As I looked both at myself and those around me, I observed tense faces, necks, shoulders, chests, and arms—psychophysical manifestations of the "upward pull" referred to by Durckheim (see the Introduction)—as many of us tried to do these exercises without the inner relaxation, sensory awareness, and muscle control that are necessary. What was amazing to me was that no one came around to help or correct us. The upward pull became even more evident when the teacher asked us to do bellows breathing, first through one nostril and then through the other. As we continued these pranayama exercises over the course of the retreat, with little visible transformation of these tensions, I began to feel that the teacher had generously overestimated the ability of many of his students to put his teaching into practice. Today, I would simply say that he had not prepared his students properly to be able to carry out such exercises in a beneficial way; he had not taken the time necessary to help them learn natural breathing.

61 *Awaken Healing Light,* pp. 173-74.

62 He discusses ways to shield the solar plexus on pp. 245-46 of *Awaken Healing Light.*

PERMISSIONS

The translation from Lao Tsu on page 9 is reprinted from *Tao Te Ching* by Lao Tsu, trans., Feng/English, Copyright © 1972 by Gia-fu Feng and Jane English. Reprinted by permission of Alfred A Knopf Inc.

The translations from Lao Tzu on pages 21 and 113 are reprinted from *The Complete Works of Lao Tzu* by Ni, Hua Ching. Reprinted by permission of Seven Star Communications, 1996.

The translation from Lao Tzu on page 84 is reprinted from *Tao Te Ching* by Lao Tzu, trans., Victor H. Mair. Reprinted by permission of Bantam Books.

The passage by Tzu Kuo Shih on page 85 is reprinted from *Qi Gong Therapy: The Chinese Art of Healing with Energy* by Tzu Kuo Shih. Reprinted by permission of Station Hill Press.

The translations from Chuang Tzu on pages 99 and 113-14 are reprinted from *Basic Writings of Chuang Tzu* edited by Burton Watson, copyright 1964 by Columbia University Press. Reprinted by permission of the publisher.

INDEX

A

abdomen, energy center in, 81–89, 155, 162–163. *See also* navel

abdominal breathing
 normal, 83–84, 90, 93, 162–163
 reverse (Taoist), 20, 84, 166–168, 183n. 32
 See also natural breathing

abdominal distention, 159

abdominal muscles, 40–42, 100, 164

abundance, 173

acceptance, 50, 51, 115

acid/alkaline balance, 36–37, 180n. 8

acquired chi, 90–91

acupuncture, 78, 148

adenoids, 32

adenosine triphosphate (ATP), 35

adrenal center, of microcosmic orbit, 150, 173

adrenal glands, 58, 173

adrenaline, 58, 62, 173

Advaita Vedanta, 15, 19

aging prematurely, 43

air
 components of, 31
 movement through respiratory system, 31–33
 quality of, 90, 104

alchemy, inner, 81, 99, 149, 155, 176

alcohol, 60

alkaline/acid balance, 36–37, 180n. 8

alternate nostril breathing, 20

alternate nostril congestion, 31–32, 180n. 6

alveoli, 33

amnesia, somatic and emotional, 48

anatomy of breathing, 29–33, 34

anger
 autonomic nervous system and, 57

health and, 14
 organs and, 132
 quality of breathing and, 55
 self-sensing and, 57
 six healing exhalations and, 158
 spacious breathing and, 126
 survival value of, 58
 venting of, 60–61

anorexia, 158

anxiety
 autoimmune diseases and, 57
 autonomic nervous system and, 57
 hyperventilation and, 54
 self-sensing and, 57
 six healing exhalations and, 159
 spaciousness and, 114
 survival value of, 58

aorta, 38

appetite loss, 132

arrogance, 158, 175

arthritis, 56, 57

asthma, 42

ATP (adenosine triphosphate), 35

attachment, 145–146

attention
 awakening, 59–60, 66–67, 84–89, 94–95
 defined, 85
 relaxation response and, 59–60
 reverse abdominal breathing and, 167, 168
 self-sensing and, 59–60, 66–67, 84–89, 94–95
 shen and, 92–95
 stress and, 59
 See also awareness; self sense

attitudes, 21, 134, 145–146, 147. *See also* self sense

autoimmune diseases, 57

autonomic nervous system, 35, 57–62

awareness
attitudes and, 21
clarity and mindfulness and, 20,
29, 92
relaxation and, 51, 65
sensory/organic
awakening, 69–73
defined, 47–48
tension and, 65, 145

See also attention; self sense; self-
sensing; spiritual growth

B

babies. *See* infants
back pain, 149, 181n. 18
bacteria, 42, 167
bad habits, 42–43, 49–50, 117
balance
breathing spaces and,
116–117, 159
energy centers and, 83, 155
healing and, 155
health and, 64
microcosmic orbit centers and,
172, 173
psychological states and, 145
See also harmony
balanced breath, 53
baraka, 77. *See also* chi
beauty, rate of breathing and, 35
being, doing vs., 62. *See also* will
bellows breathing, 163–166,
185–186n. 60
belly
opening the, 85–86, 89
outer breath and, 101, 102, 105
birth process, 27–28
bladder, 70, 137, 138, 158
Blake, William, 13
blood
circulation of, 43, 84, 90
hemoglobin, 33, 35
pH of, 36–37, 180n. 8
blood cells, 78
blood pressure, 56, 57, 132
body
historical, 47

listening to the, 51, 53
as microcosm of universe, 48–49
mind and
chemistry of connection
between, 55–57
chi and, 78–80
parasympathetic nervous system
and, 59–60

sensation of, 114–115
sensing from inside.
See self-sensing
somatic amnesia, 48
wisdom of, 47
See also organs/tissues
boredom, 53, 55
brain
breathing into, 94–95
effort and, 63–64
energy center in, 81, 92–95
massaging, 164
opening the, 94
rate of activity of, 93
relaxation and, 64–65, 90, 93
respiratory center of, 35–36
self-sensing and, 52, 53
smiling into, 138–139
stimulation of
excessive or inadequate, 60, 146
need for, 146–147

tension and, 63
See also nervous system; neuropeptides; *specific parts of brain*
brainstem, smiling into, 139
breathing
attitudes and, 21, 22
bad habits of, 42–43, 49–50, 117
as buffering mechanism, 15, 29
chest, 41–42, 54. *See also* shallow
breathing
chi and, 77
deep. *See* deep breathing
dis-ease and, 17, 42–43
ecology of, 27
emotions and, 11, 14, 17, 49, 53,
55, 134
energy and, 17, 35, 77
energy channels reopened by, 148

bubbling springs point, 106, 107
Buddha, 27, 132, 145–146, 163
Buddhism, 47, 114, 132
buffering mechanism, breathing as,
    15, 29
burdened feeling, 173, 174

C

caffeine, 60
California Pacific Medical Center, 55
calming. *See* quieting; relaxation
cancer, 56, 78
carbon, 35
carbon dioxide
    alveoli and, 33
    as component of air, 31
    hyperventilation and, 54
    negative ions and, 79
    pH of blood and, 36, 180n. 8
    plant life and, 27
    stress and, 36–37
    as waste product, 27, 35, 36–37
cautions. *See* warnings
celestial chi, 80–81, 92–95
cerebellum, 138, 139, 174
cerebral cortex, 36
cerebrospinal fluid, sensing,
    122–123, 125
channels, energy, 81, 82, 148–155
chaos, feeling a sense of, 173
chest breathing, 41–42, 54.
    See also shallow breathing
chest cavity, 29–31
chi, 77–91
    acquired, 90–91
    breath and, 77
    celestial, 80–81, 92–95
    energy of, 77, 78–80
    exercises for, 85–89, 91
    guardian, 167
    health and, 78–80, 93–94, 145
    main storage of, 171
    microcosmic orbit and, 149
    movement of, 101–103
    names for, 77
    negative ions and, 79–80
    original, 81–84

saliva and, 136, 138
three treasures and, 80–81
transformation into shen, 81, 176
triple warmer and, 116
wu, 22
Chia, Mantak, 13, 14, 18, 39, 80–82,
    90, 132, 134, 135, 149, 151, 155,
    158, 163, 171, 176
chi kung
    attention and, 85
    breathing practices and, 11, 14
    chi and, 78–79
    microcosmic orbit and, 155
    parasympathetic nervous system
        and, 181n. 18
    practices of, 78–79
    relaxation and, 181n. 18
    reverse abdominal breathing and,
        166–167
    whole-body breath and, 104
children, 11, 17, 29, 84, 99–100
Chi Nei Tsang, 13–15, 100
Chinese medicine, 48, 78, 85,
    116–117, 148, 171
ching, 80–81, 176
Christ, 27
chronic illness, 56, 60
Chuang Tzu, 99, 113–114
circulation
    of blood, 43, 84, 90
    of vital breath, 143–155
clarity, 20, 28–29, 50, 92
clavicles, 41
clavicular phase of breathing, 33
cleansing breath, 53, 162–163
CNT. *See* Chi Nei Tsang
coccyx, microcosmic orbit and, 152,
    172–173
coercion. *See* will
cold feet, 158
colds, 56, 57, 158
colon
    location of, 70
    peristalsis of, 42, 90
    sensing the, 71
    six healing exhalations and, 158
    See also constipation; irritable
    bowel syndrome

electromagnetic field, 103–104
elixir fields. *See* tan tiens
embodiment, conscious. *See* body;
  self-sensing
emotional amnesia, 48
emotions
  autonomic nervous system and,
    57–62
  biochemical correlates of, 56
  breath and, 11, 14, 17, 49, 53, 55,
    134
  Chi Nei Tsang and, 14
  defined, 132
  energy and, 14, 61, 145
  eyes and, 135
  facial expressions and, 133
  health and, 14, 60, 61, 145,
    184n. 44
  heart rate and, 57, 58, 59, 132
  hyperventilation and, 54, 179n. 3
  natural breathing and, 11, 14,
    17, 49
  negative
    abdominal muscles and, 40–41
    accepting as "normal", 60
    attention and, 59
    bellows breathing and, 166
    crown center and, 174
    diaphragm and, 39–40
    energy and, 14
    energy centers and, 83
    expansion of awareness and, 51
    expressing, 60–62
    health and, 14, 60
    hyperventilation and, 54
    microcosmic orbit centers and, 151,
    155, 171–176
    natural breathing and, 11, 14
    organs and, 40–41, 132
    physiological effects of, 58
    quality of breathing and, 54, 55
    repressing. See emotions, repressed
    sexual center and, 172
    six healing exhalations and, 158,
    159
    smiling breath and, 134, 139–140
    spaciousness and, 114
    spiritual growth and, 58

    survival value of, 58–59
    Taoism and, 61–62
    tension and, 37, 55, 58
    transforming, 61–62, 132–133
    vitality and, 60, 61–62
  observing, 68
  phases of breathing and, 33
  positive, quality of breathing
    during, 54, 55
  quieting down, 68
  repressed/suppressed, 40–41, 48,
    61, 100
  self-sensing and, 51, 53, 57–62, 73
  smiling and, 132–133
  spaciousness and, 145
  stress and, 57–62
  sympathetic nervous system and,
    57–58, 59
  tension and, 37, 55, 58, 61
  weather and, 49
  See also specific emotions
emphysema, 42, 180n. 9
emptiness, 22, 119
endorphins, 56, 64
energizing breath, 53–54
energy
  attitudes and, 21
  blockages in, 149–151
  body as microcosm of universe
    and, 49
  breathing and, 17, 35, 77
  centers of, 81–95, 155
  channels/meridians of, 81, 82,
    148–155
  cosmic, 80–81, 99
  direct sensation of, 149–155
  earth, 80–81, 99, 103, 172, 174
  effort and, 63
  emotions and, 14, 61, 145
  generator of, 172
  harmonizing overall flow of, 159
  health and, 78–80, 93–94, 145
  heredity and, 81–84
  increasing, 93, 172
  of life itself, sensation of, 115
  microcosmic orbit and, 122–123,
    147–155
  navel center and, 171

orgone, 77–78
perceptual freedom and, 64
self sense and, 115, 146
self-sensing of, 149–155
sensation of, 115
sexual, 80–81, 83, 173, 174, 176
sexual center and, 172
smiling breath and, 139
storing, 166–167, 171
subtle, 77–95
Taoism and, 18, 75–95, 99
tension wastes, 145
universal, 80–81
Western science and, 77
See also chi
enzymes, 64, 78. *See also* pepsin
epiglottis, 34
Esalen Institute, 47
esophagus, 32, 38
exercises. *See* breathing exercises
exhalation
anatomy of, 29, 31, 32, 33, 35–36,
39, 102
balancing with inhalation, 53
distinguishing from inhalation,
100–103
emphasizing inhalation over,
53–54
emphasizing over inhalation, 53
inner and outer breath and,
100–103, 105–106
pause between inhalation and, 123
phases of breathing and, 33
psychological obstacles to full,
118, 119
quality of, 54–55
self-sensing and, 49
significance of, 17, 27, 49
six healing exhalations, 157,
158–159
spaciousness and, 121–122
exhaustion. *See* fatigue
extensor muscles, 37
eyes, 135, 158

F

face, relaxing the, 125, 133, 135–136

fatigue, 43, 51, 53, 117, 166
fear
autoimmune diseases and, 57
autonomic nervous system and, 57
avoidance of feeling, 15
birth process and, 27–28
of change, 172
diaphragm and, 39–40
health and, 14
hyperventilation and, 54
microcosmic orbit centers and,
172, 173
organs and, 132
quality of breathing during, 54, 55
self-sensing and, 57
six healing exhalations and, 158
solar plexus and, 90
See also panic
feelings. *See* emotions
feet
cold, 158
making contact with the, 106
Feldenkrais, Moshe, 63, 132
Feldenkrais method, 19
fight or flight reflex, 41, 54, 57, 124,
135, 173
following the breath, 50–51, 69
food
chi acquired from, 90
immune system and, 146–147
as stimulation, 60
freedom, feeling a sense of, 173,
176
functional channel, 148–149,
153–154

G

gall bladder, 158
generosity, 173
glands, smiling into, 132
golden elixir, 136
gossip, 83
governor channel, 148–149, 152–153
grief, 158
Grof, Stanislov, 179n. 3
groundedness, 172
guardian chi, 167

hormones, 64, 78, 84
Huang Ti, 18
humanity, feeling a sense of, 174
human potential movement, 47
humor, 131. *See also* smiling breath
Hymes, Alan, 33
hyperactivity, 173
hypertension, 56, 132
hyperventilation
  anxiety and, 54
  bellows breathing and, 165
  as breathing exercise, 20, 179n. 3
  defined, 54
  emotions and, 54, 179n. 3
  stress and poorly functioning
    diaphragm and, 41
hypothalamus, 138, 139, 174

I

identification, 145–146
illness. *See* dis-ease
illusions, 174
immune system, 55–57
  autoimmune diseases, 57
  chi and, 79
  guardian chi and, 167
  heart center and, 175
  reverse abdominal breathing and,
    167
  self-sensing and, 55–57
  smiling breath and, 134
  stimulation nourishes, 146–147
  thoughts and feelings and, 55–56,
    184n. 44
impatience, 55, 126, 158, 175. *See
  also* patience
impressions, need for new, 145–147,
  172
infants, 11, 17, 29, 84
infections, 42, 43
inhalation
  anatomy of, 29, 31, 32, 33, 35–36,
    38–39, 102
  balancing with exhalation, 53
  emphasizing exhalation over, 53
  over exhalation, 53–54
  inner and outer breath and,

100–103, 105–106
  pause between exhalation and,
    123
  phases of breathing and, 33
  psychological obstacles to full,
    118–119
  quality of, 54–55
  self-sensing and, 49
  significance of, 17, 27, 49
  spaciousness and, 121–122, 123
inner alchemy, 81, 99, 149, 155, 176
inner breath, 35, 100–103, 106
inner growth. *See* spiritual growth
inner quieting, 65–69
inner smile, 131–132, 134, 135. *See
  also* smiling breath
insecurity, 172
insomnia. *See* sleep disorders
inspiration, feeling a sense of, 174
integral awareness. *See* self-sensing
intercostal muscles, 29, 30, 31,
  32, 35
intestines. *See* colon; constipation;
  irritable bowel syndrome; small
  intestine
intuition, 92, 175
irritable bowel syndrome, 56

J

jade pillow, microcosmic orbit and,
  152, 174
James, William, 132
jealousy, 158
Jesus Christ, 27
joy, 175
judgmentalism, 83, 90.
  See also criticism

K

kidney center, of microcosmic orbit,
  150, 152, 173
kidneys
  cleansing and energizing, 88–89
  referral of pain in, 71
  sensing the, 71
  six healing exhalations and, 158

smiling into, 137, 138
Taoism and, 49
kindness, 55

L

lactic acid, 37
Lao Tzu, 9, 21, 27, 49, 84, 113, 155
large intestine. *See* colon
large orbit, 155
larynx, 32, 34
laughter, 131. *See also* smiling breath
laws
    law of least effort, 63–64
    of life, 49
    of nature, 18
    Weber-Fechner psychophysical law,
        63
letting go, 19, 118, 119. *See also*
    relaxation
life force. *See* chi; energy; vitality
listening to the body, 51, 53
listlessness, 172, 173
liver
    location of, 70
    sensing the, 71, 72
    six healing exhalations and, 158
    smiling into, 136–138
    solar plexus center and, 176
    Taoism and, 49
loneliness, 172
longevity, 18, 80, 85
love, 55, 90, 175
Lowen, Alexander, 99
lower back
    opening the, 88–89
    pain in, 181n. 18
lower breathing space, 116–117,
    120–121, 159
lung (Tibetan term), 77. *See also* chi
lungs
    anatomy of breathing and, 29–31,
        32, 33, 34, 38–39, 101, 102
    bad breathing habits and, 42
    compensating for decreased space
        in, 41–42
    location of, 70
    natural breathing and, 11

phases of breathing and, 33
sensing the, 71
six healing exhalations and, 158
smiling into, 136, 137
Taoism and, 49
waste elimination through, 42
lymphatic system, 42, 84, 163–164

M

macrocosmic orbit, 155
Marin, Gilles, 13–14
massage
    of brain, 164
    energy channels reopened by, 148
    of organs, 13, 38, 60, 83–84, 164
May, Rollo, 51
meaning, need for, 146
mechanics of breathing, 25–43
    anatomy of breathing, 29–33, 34
    bad habits, 42–43, 49–50, 117
    birth process and, 27–28
    clarity and, 28–29
    exhaling. *See* exhalation
    expanding the self sense and, 27
    inhaling. *See* inhalation
    inner breath and, 35, 106
    mindfulness and, 28–29
    phases of breathing, 33–34
    rate of breathing. *See* rate of
        breathing
    respiratory center and, 35–36
    respiratory muscles and.
        See respiratory muscles
    respiratory system and, 29–33
    volume of breath, 31, 38–39
meditation, 78, 80, 148
medulla oblongata, 35, 36, 38, 174
memory
    sacral center and, 172, 173
    self-sensing vs., 47, 48
menstrual disorders, 159
meridians, 81, 82, 148–155
metabolism, 39, 49
microcosmic orbit
    cerebrospinal fluid sensing and,
        122–123
    psychological dimensions of, 151,

Westerners and, 19–20
See also breathing exercises;
letting go
repetition, self-sensing vs., 48
repressed emotions, 40–41, 48, 61,
100
respect, 175
respiratory center, 35–36
respiratory illnesses, 43
respiratory muscles, 37–42
diaphragm. *See* diaphragm
extensor muscles, 37
intercostal muscles, 29, 30, 31,
32, 35
psoas muscles, 37
respiratory system, 29–33
rest, rate of breathing and, 29, 36
retention of breath, 20, 27, 36
reverse breathing
Taoist abdominal, 20, 84, 166–168,
183n. 32
vital breath circulation and, 154
rheumatoid arthritis, 57
ribs
anatomy of breathing and, 29, 30,
31, 32, 34, 38, 41–42
opening the rib cage, 72, 87, 89
risk-taking, 176
Rossi, Ernest, 59
ruach, 77. *See also* chi

S

sacrum, microcosmic orbit and, 150,
152, 172–173
sadness, 14, 158
saliva, 136, 138
science, Western, energy and, 77
self-confidence, 173
self-healing
natural breathing and, 20, 49
self-sensing and, 50, 51
smiling breath and, 134
tan tien cleansing breath and, 162
Taoism and, 80
self-image. *See* self sense
self-judgment, 55
self-knowledge, 52–53, 56–57

self-pity, 93, 126, 175
self-respect, 175
self sense
attachment/identification and,
145–146
attitudes and, 21
bad breathing habits and, 49–50,
117
energy and, 115, 146
expanding the
*breathing and, 21, 22, 27, 49,
50–51, 104–105*
*healing and wholeness and, 21–22,
145, 155*
levels of sensation and, 115, 123
lower energy center and, 155
navel center and, 172
need for, 145–147
overview of, 21–22
perceptual reeducation and, 49–50
smiling and, 133
spaciousness and, 115
going beyond the, 115, 123
See also self-sensing
self-sensing, 47–73
as acceptance of what is, 50, 51, 115
actions and senses and, 52
attention and, 59–60, 66–67,
84–89, 94–95
body as microcosm of universe
and, 48–49
defined, 47–48
effects of, 48, 52–53
effortless effort and, 62–64
emotions and, 51, 53, 57–62, 73
of energy, 149–155
energy centers and, 155
exercises for, 43, 65–69, 71–73,
84–89, 105–109
following the breath, 50–51, 69
health and, 47, 48, 56–57, 65
immune system and, 55–57
importance to breathwork, 19, 20,
47, 84–85
inhalation and exhalation and, 49
inner and outer breath and, 72,
100–103, 105–106
levels of, 114–115, 123

listening to the body, 51, 53
microcosmic orbit centers and,
151
nervous system and, 52–53, 57–62
new impressions and, 147, 172
organs and, 69–73
perceptual freedom and, 64–65
perceptual reeducation and,
49–50, 53
quality of breathing and, 54–55
self-knowledge and, 52–53, 56–57
self-transformation and, 52–53
smiling breath and, 134
spaciousness and, 115
spiritual growth and, 47, 48
tension and, 65, 145
three kinds of breath and, 53–54
whole-body breath and, 104–105
wholeness and, 50
will vs., 48, 62–64
self-transformation, self-sensing and,
52–53
Selver, Charlotte, 47
sensing oneself. *See* self-sensing
sensory awareness. *See* awareness,
sensory/organic; self-sensing
sensory cortex, 52
septum, 31
serotonin, negative ions and, 79
sexual activity
energy centers and, 83
as stimulation, 60
sexual center, of microcosmic orbit,
150, 152, 153, 172
sexual disorders, 43, 158
sexual essence, 80–81, 83, 173, 174,
176
sexual organs, smiling into, 137, 138
shallow breathing, 15, 17, 41–42,
54, 100
shen, 80–81, 92–95, 176
sighing, 53
silence, 22, 51, 114, 119.
See also quieting; stillness
sinus congestion, 158
sitting position, 67–68
six healing exhalations, 157,
158–159

size of breath, 31, 38–39
skeletal structure, 40. *See also* spine
sleep disorders
bad breathing habits and, 43
emotions and, 132
six healing exhalations and, 158,
159
stress and, 56
small brain center. *See* jade pillow
small intestine
location of, 70
peristalsis of, 42, 90
sensing the, 71, 72
See also irritable bowel syndrome
small orbit. *See* microcosmic orbit
smiling
chemistry of, 131–134
healing and, 131, 133–134
inner smile, 131–132, 134, 135
voluntary vs. involuntary, 132–133
smiling breath, 129–140
smoking, 60
sneezing, 31
Sobel, David, 79, 146
solar plexus
abdominal breathing and, 90
energy center in, 81, 90–91
microcosmic orbit and, 150, 152,
153, 176
opening the, 91
somatic amnesia, 48
sore throat, 159
sound, breathing exercise using,
158–159
spaces, breathing, 115–117,
120–121, 123, 159
spacious breath, 111–127
inner smile and, 134, 136, 138–139
spaciousness, 113–115, 117,
121–122, 123, 145
speech. *See* talking
spine
diaphragm and, 40
lengthening, 107–109
parasympathetic nervous system
and, 59, 181n. 18
releasing tension in, 181n. 18
sensing breath of, 122–123

trachea, 31, 32, 34, 101
transformation. *See* alchemy; self-transformation
triple warmer, 116–117, 159
trust, 54

U

ulcers, 43, 56, 158, 159
ultradian rhythm, 31–32, 180n. 6
universal force, 80–81, 99, 103
unknown, embracing the, 119
upper breathing space, 116–117, 120–121, 159
upward pull, 19, 186n. 60.
    See also will
uterus, referral of pain in, 71

V

vagus nerve, 35, 38, 59
vena cava, 38
vertigo, 158
victim, feeling of being a, 174
vigilant relaxation, 64
viruses, 42, 167
visualization, neuropeptides and, 56
vital breath, circulating the, 143–155
vitality
    adrenal center and, 173
    artificially induced, 19
    attitudes and, 21
    breathing and, 17
    chi as, 81
    diaphragm and, 39
    kidney center and, 173
    negative emotions and, 60, 61–62
    self-sensing and new impressions and, 147
    sexual essence and, 83, 173
    six healing exhalations and, 158
    spaciousness and, 115
    tan tien cleansing breath and, 162
    See also chi; energy
volume of breath, 31, 38–39

W

warnings, about breathing exercises, 19–21, 155, 183n. 32
weather, emotions and, 49
Weber-Fechner psychophysical law, 63
well-being. *See* health
Westerners
    energy and, 77
    will and relaxation and, 19–20
wheel of life. *See* microcosmic orbit
whole-body breath, 97–109
wholeness
    all-inclusive, 22
    breathing and, 17, 27, 62
    healing and, 13–14, 21, 50
    health and, 80
    perceptual reeducation and, 49–50, 51
    self sense and, 21–22, 145, 155
    going beyond the self sense, 115, 123
    self-sensing and, 50
    spaciousness and, 115
will
    effortless effort vs., 62–64
    negative effects of, 19, 185–186n. 60
    self-sensing vs., 48, 62–64
    Westerners and, 19–20, 28
wisdom of body, 47
wonder, 55, 115
worry, 83, 90, 126, 159, 176
wu chi, 22

XYZ

yang channel. *See* governor channel
yang and yin. *See* yin and yang
yawning, 53
yin channel. *See* functional channel
yin and yang
    breathing and, 27, 157
    defined, 22
    energy of life itself and, 115
    health and, 64